Conversations
with Toni Cade Bambara

Literary Conversations Series
Peggy Whitman Prenshaw
General Editor

Conversations
with Toni Cade Bambara

Edited by Thabiti Lewis

University Press of Mississippi   Jackson

Books by Toni Cade Bambara

The Black Woman: An Anthology. New York: New American Library, 1970; New York: Washington Square Press, 2005.

Tales and Stories for Black Folks. New York: Zenith Books, 1971.

Gorilla, My Love. New York: Random House, 1972; New York: Vintage Books, 1992.

The Sea Birds Are Still Alive: Collected Stories. New York: Random House, 1977.

The Salt Eaters. New York: Random House, 1980; New York: Vintage Books, 1992.

Deep Sightings and Rescue Missions: Fiction, Essays, and Conversations. New York: Pantheon Books, 1996; New York: Vintage Books, 1999.

Those Bones Are Not My Child. New York: Pantheon Books, 1999; New York: Vintage Books, 2000.

Films

The Bombing of Osage Avenue (documentary, 1986)

W. E. B. Du Bois: A Biography in Four Voices (documentary, co-directed by Louis J. Massiah, 1995)

www.upress.state.ms.us

The University Press of Mississippi is a member of the Association of American University Presses.

First printing 2012
∞
Library of Congress Cataloging-in-Publication Data
Bambara, Toni Cade.
Conversations with Toni Cade Bambara / edited by Thabiti Lewis.
      p. cm. — (Literary conversations series)
   Includes index.
ISBN: 978-1-4968-1307-7   1. Bambara, Toni Cade—Interviews. 2.
Authors, American—20th century—Interviews. I. Lewis, Thabiti. II. Title.
   PS3552.A473Z46 2012
   813'.54—dc23 [B]   2011026503

British Library Cataloging-in-Publication Data available

Contents

Introduction

Toni Cade Bambara, a multi-talented filmmaker, writer, serious activist, and teacher died of colon cancer December 9, 1995, in Philadelphia. The life she lived was one that made significant contributions in African American literature, culture, independent film, and feminism. Bambara's longtime friend and editor, Toni Morrison, proclaimed Bambara's writing to be "absolutely critical to twentieth-century literature" (Boyd 91). Further, she described Bambara as "an unreconstructed rebel—I mean, beautiful in every aspect of that . . . [she] was just outrageously brilliant" (91). Undeniably, Bambara was an "unreconstructed rebel"; those who knew her would concur. This assessment resonates in her work as she displayed a penchant for extending the limits of language, narrator roles, and narrative structure. Her acts of literary extension were derived from her sentiments, as expressed in *The Black Woman*, that "we are involved in a struggle for liberation: liberation from the exploited and dehumanizing system of racism . . . liberation from the constrictive norms of 'mainstream' culture; from the synthetic myths that encourage us to fashion ourselves visibly from without (reaction) rather than from within (creation) . . . and a turning towards each other" (7). Moreover, the primary audience that she identified with and felt it was her duty to serve are regular folk she encountered in the streets, on buses, trains, or laundry mats. Indeed, the conversations with academics, filmmakers, poets, and scholars that follow reflect these sentiments, as well as other important insights into her political sensibilities, writing craft, and commitment to being an unreconstructed artist of and for the people. Bambara was capable of and interested in writing what she termed "straight-up fiction."[1] As a general rule she considered it "rude" to write autobiographically. The interviews collected in this volume accurately echo the interests and the focus of a writer who understands the importance of negotiating serious feminist views, while also prioritizing African American cultural, linguistic, and general community concerns. Indeed, Bambara champions the everyday folk; she celebrates struggle and *all* who are part of it—from the artistic to the political to the person on the corner.

In some circles the literary interview is considered an amalgamation of sorts because it blurs boundaries of journalism, history, and everyday conversation. But when the subject is Toni Cade Bambara, perhaps the most appropriate expression of the whole of her personality—the unique passion, ideology, and perspective that resists categorization—is through a hybrid vehicle. What better way to represent an artist with an interdisciplinary vision that embraced amalgamation, yet blurred while deftly negotiating and balancing boundaries of fact, fiction, feminism, nationalism, music, and film? The opulence and intimacy of these collaborations or conversations between Bambara and her interviewers is an excellent and necessary resource for those interested in pragmatic as well as scholarly approaches to her fiction, especially her novels *The Salt Eaters* (1980) and *Those Bones Are Not My Child* (1999). The passion, humor, and genius of the woman behind the work are revealed in these discussions.

It is impossible to categorize her as simply a woman of letters. Like many of the women and girls depicted in her fiction, she too was a community worker, teacher, and leader. The only difference is that she also happened to be a writer. Which is why it is not surprising that when interviewer Kay Bonetti pressed Bambara to describe herself as a writer, Bambara explained that she had " . . . always thought of [herself] as a teacher who writes, a social worker who writes, a youth worker who writes, a mother who writes."[2] Nor is it surprising that she told Askasha Hull she viewed her vocation to be organizing, writing, and raising her child. Ironically each of these personas—teacher, social worker, youth worker, writer—find space and voice in her fiction. While she certainly wrote short stories, novels, poetry, plays, essays, and screenplays, it was film that was, in fact, her first love. But she always found a way to incorporate aspects of cinema into her fiction, whether via direct references to film or through use of cinematic transitions and descriptions—a device that guides readers through her two novels *The Salt Eaters* (1980) and *Those Bones Are Not My Child* (1999). In fact, after completing her novels, film became the medium of choice to convey the ineffable details of life she found difficult to convey as a writer.

Besides her passion for cinema, community work was her life's passion, and writing was what she did to remain sane. Often she used her skills as a writer to serve the community, holding writing workshops in her home to provide an outlet for people to learn to express themselves. Once when a course she was scheduled to teach was canceled by the university she was working at in Atlanta, undeterred she unofficially conducted the course from her home! The woman's spirit was one that could not be controlled. Bambara, a self-described "product of the sixties spirit," unquestionably viewed herself as a cultural worker for oppressed people whose job as an artist was making "revolution irresistible." Indeed, her fiction usually found a way to champion and empower the powerless child, old person, woman, the working class, "average" folk, and cultural workers—invisible voices in our society. As she explained in the preface to *Gorilla, My Love* (1972), she dealt in "straight-up fiction . . . 'cause [she] value[d] family and friends."[3] Clearly her fiction confirms that her strength and growth as a writer stems from her gift, her magnificent ability to transmute what has come to her one way into something else.

Early in her career Bambara enjoyed literary success when she assembled a collection of black feminist voices in the earth-shattering feminist anthology *The Black Woman* (1970). She will forever be remembered for displaying foresight and courage to organize this very important book. It was a significant accomplishment, for it was published at a time when there was a definite void of such works. The impetus for the project emerged from Bambara's impatience with the serious void in writing for African American women or by African American women in the 1960s. In retrospect, the book is monumental because it lobbied for a radical agenda for women's studies, rights, or realities that placed black women at the center of many feminist debates.

The eclectic assembly of women in *The Black Woman* foreshadowed the global or multicultural/multiethnic women's movement Bambara would advocate throughout her life. Bambara's vision was never narrowly focused on the crimes of white patriarchy; it was also critical of any version of radical black struggle and nationalism that was hindered by patriarchal heterosexists paradigms. What is evident in her fiction and activist vision is that her frames of reference transcend gender and race such that her feminist focus is international in scope and somewhat transracial (quite evident in *The Salt Eaters* and *The Sea Birds Are Still Alive*). And yet Bambara's literary and cultural contribution has been underappreciated. Perhaps this oversight occurs because of her propinquity to writers such as Morrison and Walker. However, whatever the cause, not nearly enough attention has been given to her significance or her groundbreaking contributions to feminist theory and African American literature. Perhaps what made her subsequent work so unique, so visionary was her deft "pre-womanist" ability to negotiate nationalism and feminism. In fact, this creative genius radiates from several of her works of fiction and even essays like "On the Issue of Roles."

Toni Cade Bambara was born Miltona Mirkin Cade on March 25,1939, to Helen Cade Brehon and Walter Cade II.[4] They lived in Harlem for the first ten years of her life. It is this same Harlem community populated by "Miss Naomi, Miss Gladys, and life-women" that she credits with having a significant influence on her writing and life. When reading her first collection of short fiction, *Gorilla, My Love* (1972), the sights, smells, politics, and people of her Harlem youth, along with the rhythms of bebop drive nearly every story. When reflecting upon how she came to be, she always spoke fondly of "living on 151st Street between Broadway and Amsterdam," absorbing the jazz music "of the forties and fifties" and the culture of the Apollo Theatre with her father, and hearing from Speakers Corner the arguments of trade unionists, Rastas, and Pan-Africanists.[5] She credits as critical to her early development the many life and cultural lessons learned while living among the diverse population of her neighborhood. These experiences shaped her unique vision of wholeness that embraced nationalist black activism and feminist-based black liberation struggle that is prominently featured in her fiction.

While her parents and members of her childhood neighborhood are lauded for being instrumental in shaping part of her identity,[6] her mother Helen receives special credit for providing her space to think and dream; so much room that the young Miltona felt free to change her name to "Toni" before she entered first grade.[7] In fact, her respect for her mother can also be gauged by her mom's contribution of a historical reflective essay, "Looking Back," in Bambara's important anthology *The Black Woman* (1970). The essay details the love, hate, confusion, need, pride, and embarrassment of being a black woman in different eras from 1915 to the 1960s in "white America, a capitalist democracy." That Bambara valued her mother's generational perspective and her wisdom enough to have her contribute to this anthology as an anchoring voice of sorts says much about the respect she held for her mother and elders in general. In addition to her parents and community Bambara also credited her editor and close friend, Toni Morrison, as an important influence, and Morrison might say the same about Bambara. In addition to Morrison, Bambara also credits the literary influence of writers like Quincy Troupe, Camille Yarborough, Jayne Ortiz, Ida B. Wells, Sean Wong, and Charat Chandra for inspiring her to develop her sense of experiment and tradition.

To understand Bambara's evolution into a premiere black woman writer capable of producing fiction that negotiates the ideals of Black Nationalism without sacrificing her commitment to feminism requires revisiting her early adulthood. Toni Cade graduated from Queen's College in 1959. She received a B.A. in theater arts and English.[8] Six years later Bambara completed her master's degree (1965). While completing her degree she was the program director at Colony Settlement House in Brooklyn.[9] The confluence of these experiences is ubiquitous in focus and form of her early hip short stories like "The Lesson," "The Hammer Man," and "Raymond's Run" in *Gorilla, My Love*. Although she writes "straight-up fiction," the tough little kids are more than figments of her imagination but at least inspired by real people or events she may have encountered during this era of her life.

After receiving her master's she taught at City College of New York where she worked for four years. It was during this period that Bambara says she became involved in different sociopolitical issues and community groups—something she would continue to do throughout her life wherever she resided.[10] Although City College seemed to be a satisfying experience, Bambara later was offered and accepted a position as assistant professor at Livingston College (at Rutgers) where she immediately connected with the students and the black community in the area.[11] She was more than a teacher but a mentor and friend to students and members of the community.

The trajectory of Bambara's creative projects throughout her career reveal a woman who refused to separate the struggle for civil rights from a commitment to women's struggle for freedom. This was immediately clear in 1970 when she published the anthology *The Black Woman* under the name Toni Cade, and shortly thereafter changed to Toni Cade Bambara. Similar to much 1970s feminist criticism, her anthology focused on images of women and the connection of those images to women's oppression. Her book was unique and diverged from other similar works because it was firmly rooted in the diverse experience of black women, both celebrating that experience and critiquing popular stereotypes. *The Black Woman* received enormous acclaim. As Eleanor Traylor points out in her introduction of the reissued edition, the anthology "pluck[ed] the 'weasel' of thought and fire[d] the pistol of action" and emerged "as a founding text of a 'womanist' evolutionary enunciation" (Traylor x). Indeed, the collection was necessary and masterful. And, as Traylor aptly contends, its prevailing power stems from the "voices [that . . .] were (and remain) active participants in an ever-evolving movement whose impact at mid-twentieth century was perhaps the most revolutionary cultural and intellectual reimagining to have occurred in the United States since the birth of America in The Declaration of Independence" (xii).

On the heels of the success of *The Black Woman*, Bambara edited an anthology of short stories, *Tales and Stories for Black Folks* (1971), which was also well received. This anthology was unique in that it included short stories from students in her creative writing courses at Livingston College (at Rutgers University) alongside of established writers. The intended audience was high school and college students, but it proved to have broader appeal. The book included a section with stories by Langston Hughes, Ernest J. Gaines, Pearl Crayton, and Alice Walker. Several of the stories in the book fall under the category Bambara calls "Our Great Kitchen Tradition." The book itself reflected her belief in valuing multiple voices and perspectives of the known and unknown.

The following year Bambara's first collection of short stories, and perhaps her most famous (most of them written between 1950 and 1970), *Gorilla, My Love* (1972), was published and received favorable reviews. The stories echoed feminist and nationalist ideals with the same focus, seriousness, wit, and balance that she had previously articulated in the essay "On the Issue of Roles" found in her anthology *The Black Woman*, where she echoed her famous vision of gender: ". . . I am neither a man nor a woman who wishes to be a man—I tend to find no particularly rigid work assignment based on sex" (Bambara 124). Accepting constraints in any aspect of her life was just not an option for Bambara. This essay, published four decades ago, is a precursor to what would later be termed "Womanism" by Alice Walker in the 1980s. Bambara's early iteration of "Womanism" simultaneously negotiated inclusion for community, youth, elders, feminism, and Black Nationalism.

Gorilla, My Love, which contains fifteen stories including her humorous "A Sort of Preface," extends the vision and strong feminist voices articulated in *The Black Woman*. The stories are set in the rural South as well as the North. They examine an array of relationships in ways that reposition female voices to the forefront—young and old, conservative and loose. An important recurring theme in the collection is the necessity for black women to support and nurture each other, and heal each other's inner wounds.

The book features black women and girls whose individuality and resistance to conformity encourages heroism and discards marginality. The book was enthusiastically reviewed as an example of portraits of black life that focused on love and created memorable characters. With the publication and subsequent success of *Gorilla, My Love*, coupled with her enormously popular anthology *The Black Woman* a few years earlier, Bambara solidified her reputation as a leading Black Nationalist, feminist, and social activist.

After the publication of *Gorilla, My Love*, she visited Cuba in 1973 where she met with women's organizations and women workers. This trip inspired her to think more seriously about the connection between writing and social activism, as well as about possibilities for women in the United States.

She tells ya Salaam: "I think it was in 1973 when I really began to realize this [writing] was a perfectly legitimate way to participate in struggle . . . This counts too."[12] It would become a signature emphasis in her subsequent fiction and personal activity. As more international organizations became aware of her work and purpose she received an invitation to visit Vietnam as a guest of the Women's Union in 1975. The impact of this visit seems to resonate in her second collection of short fiction, *The Sea Birds Are Still Alive* (1977), which is filled with strong feminist voices that depict local and international struggles of women seeking equality and contributing significantly as community workers and organizers. This particular body of work was also a testament of her broadening vision of feminist struggle, foreshadowing the vision of wholeness she would display in subsequent fiction. Prior to and perhaps in the process of composing *The Sea Birds*, Bambara traveled widely, visiting various countries as a member of delegations (from Laos to Vietnam).

A major focus in *The Seabirds Are Still Alive* is social activism in the form of female possibilities, community organizing, and overcoming the injustices leveled upon women and children while extending notions of Third World coalitions. *The Seabirds Are Still Alive* is Bambara's triumph of her belief in using writing as a tool of social activism, for this collection has a geopolitical feminist tone. It also previews her interest in human transformation and revolutionary change—wholeness that is a primary focus of her first novel. Nearly every story in *The Seabirds Are Still Alive* reveals her enormous gift of storytelling; a gift that allows her to encompass some aspect of social and political change without sacrificing her art. Indeed this collection of stories reinforced her conviction that there was an art to telling stories bound in political and social issues that required true artistic talent.

Not long after giving birth to her only daughter, Karma Cade, she relocated to Atlanta, where she began writing her first novel, *The Salt Eaters* (1980). This novel extends the notion of using storytelling to effect social change to even greater heights. The acclaimed work focuses on a community that has lost its way, and Velma Henry who experiences both mental and emotional crisis, and Minnie Ransom, a faith healer who helps make her whole.

As with much of her life, this novel avoids linear trajectory, opting instead for a more inclusive circular narrative pattern; the novel employs nearly seamless shifts of time and place to trace the journey of the main character, Velma Henry—and in fact her entire community—toward healing and wholeness. Bambara successfully experiments with narrative voice and language as few before her had done in fiction. A technique that she described as telling "the truth" by inventing "new forms, new modes, and new idioms" (ya Salaam 48).

The unique quality of *The Salt Eaters* is that it revealed Bambara's burgeoning interest in exploring a different kind of medium, as well as the expansiveness of her repertoire of rhetorical skills. She takes language and traditional notions of the role and status of the narrator to new heights, making the novel represent a distinct shift from more linear narrative structure that was common at the time. To achieve this somewhat perplexing method Bambara claims that while writing she was "in a state of altered consciousness in the sense that [she is] self-remembering . . . I am acutely aware of dialogue that is going on between me and the characters which are conjured. I am acutely aware of myself as reader. I actually am aware of the relationship between what's going on in my head and what I can do with my hands" (ya Salaam 49).

The novel also interrogates notions of female spirituality and wholeness via social activism, individual mental and physical health, community well-being, and personal and collective history, as well as the many roots and branches of a spirituality necessary to hold together what Bambara considers to be the primarily dissipated and fractured energies of the 1960s and 1970s movements for social change. Some reviewers criticized the fast pace and numerous characters, but Bambara explains that the pace and multiple characters allow her to fuse the activists, warriors, and medicine people into a venerable force (50–51) capable of forming a coalition because they recognize they have a common agenda—liberation.

Bambara's frustrations with developing this new status as not quite narrator but more of a guide or medium in fiction explain her explicit revelation in several interviews that film is her preferred medium of expression. She seems to prefer this medium because of the visual story she can convey with the camera and script that is not readily accessible in fiction. Thus, in her later interviews she makes clear that she prefers to be known first and foremost as a filmmaker.[13] This also explains why Bambara relocated from Atlanta to Philadelphia where she met Louis Massiah, founder-director of the Scribe Video Center, and started making documentary films.

In Philadelphia working with Massiah at Scribe Center, she improved her editing and her documentary filmmaking skills, and she even became involved in teaching others about filmmaking. During a conversation with Massiah in 2003 at his Philadelphia home, he revealed to me that when he met Bambara she possessed considerable knowledge about film. Although Bambara humbly contends she learned much from working with Massiah, it appears that she knew more about film before coming to Philadelphia than she lets on in her interviews.

One of the first film projects she was involved with in Philadelphia was the extremely important documentary *The Bombing of Osage Avenue* (1986), which won the Best Documentary Academy Award. The film is about the May 13, 1985, bombing of the headquarters of the black organization, MOVE, in Philadelphia's Cobb's Creek neighborhood.[14] Bambara conducted many interviews for this film and recorded eyewitness accounts. She went into the streets, among the people—an easy thing for her—to give them an opportunity to voice their perspective of what happened that day and leading up to the unfortunate incident. This is what Bambara was all about; it was quite natural for her to interview the unheard voices of the community. Bambara seemed to be drawn to film, particularly this documentary project, because she believed it to be a great medium to give voice to the people and expose truth, particularly the brutality and inhumanity of an event that caused the death of at least eleven people and the destruction of an entire community.[15] By the late 1980s Bambara had turned her focus primarily to film, admitting as much during her dialogue with Akasha Hull.[16]

In an interview with Kay Bonetti, Bambara reflected on her artistry in this manner: "When I look back at my work with any little distance, the two characteristics that jump out at me is one, the tremendous capacity for laughter, but also a tremendous capacity for rage."[17] Indeed this is a wonderful assessment of her work; the rage came from the injustices she saw in the treatment of children, the elderly, women, and the oppressed black community. Also during the Kay Bonetti interview, Bambara ponders the symbolism of salt and the African flying myth, both critical metaphorical components to her first novel. She explains, "We got grounded because we ate too much salt, but some folks say we got grounded because we opened ourselves up to horror—invited it onto the continent—that created tears. And it was that salt that drowned our wings and made us earth-bound."[18] Bambara sought to function as "a new kind of narrator—narrator as medium . . . a kind of magnet through which other people tell their stories."[19] A careful review of her fiction reveals Black Arts Movement influences that emphasized producing art by, for, and of the people, which led her to actively seek a narrator/medium role in her art. Functioning as a narrator/medium the folk—past and present—become visible in her fiction. Her writing was beautifully political, a seemingly effortless balance of ornate and simple language that was organic. She amplified multiple community voices simultaneously, capturing all the divergent register of voices, issues, idioms, riddles, intonations, and vocabulary of the African American community much like a jazz musician playing bebop.

The Salt Eaters (1980) is a very complex, multilayered, and multiperspective novel. Some readers unfamiliar with African American literary traditions can become overwhelmed with sorting out Bambara's impetus and narrative voice, or tracking the myriad flashbacks and the array of individuals floating throughout the book. Most readers become frustrated trying to discern which narrative lines to follow, or the registers that her characters speak on. Bambara's moderator or narrator/medium navigates a narrative structure that traipses different characters' life registers and never-before-explored dimensions, which can make completing the novel quite difficult.[20] This collection of Bambara's conversations offers casual readers and scholars some sound direction regarding what it is that she thinks she is doing as an artist. She explains the traditions, spirituality, politics, wisdoms, and artistry that drive her work.

Bambara's fiction is remarkable and has had a huge impact on contemporary American literature, not just African American literature. One outstanding trait in her work is an ability to display a high level of musicality. Also, she fuses vernacular humor with experimental impulses with great ease. Furthermore, her notions of feminism laid an early framework for "womanist" ideals. In fact, what is unique about Bambara's feminist agenda was her willingness to remain critical of patriarchy without excluding men or their issues from her narratives. It is for these reasons that her literary vision is so important. A cursory glance at her essays and fiction reveal a literary voice that is intent on being balanced or whole, committed to depictions that nudge the gender politics dialogue in the most honorable and productive direction. Whenever Bambara discusses her fiction she is always mindful of social activism and Black Aesthetics of the 1970s. One pattern or idea that emerges in the interviews is her Afrocentric and feminist interests that draw on black narrative folklore, jazz, and spiritual traditions that assist her never-ending search for a "spiritually whole" representation of African American literature and culture.

The conversations assembled here provide a sort of road map into the very intelligent and complicated mind of Toni Cade Bambara, who negotiated feminism and Black Nationalism, and championed the voice of the folk in a new language, with cinematic influences. The interviews with Beverly Guy-Sheftall, Kalamu ya Salaam, Kay Bonetti, Claudia Tate, Louis Massiah, Justine Tally, Gloria Hull, and Zala Chandler are a necessary tool for those who want to understand better the why and how of Bambara the writer,

teacher, activist, and filmmaker. Without a doubt, these conversations provide insight into her artistry, politics, and aesthetic sensibilities. Examined
as a whole, they unfold her vision as a writer in search of truth, always serious, and challenging the unjust. For example, during her interview with
Guy-Sheftall she recapitulates sentiments from her landmark essay "On the
Issue of Roles" regarding gender and politics. With Sheftall she also discusses craft, feminism, and what it means for her to be a writer, confidently
declaring that she is not hemmed by "contradiction or tensions between
being a feminist, being a pan-Africanist, being a black nationalist, being an
internationalist, being a socialist, and being a woman in North America"
(Sheftall in *Savoring the Salt* 117).

Meanwhile, her conversation with Kalamu ya Salaam reveals her quest
for a language that speaks the tongue of African American communities;
one that adequately translates the visions and reality, the present and future
onto the page at the same time. She muses about her efforts to "break words
open and get at the bases, deal with symbols as though they were atoms."
Indeed, she discusses her search for a language or "mother tongue" in her
fiction as a tongue or voice that adequately allows people to validate that
experience, and tell the truth.[21]

Claudia Tate's interview with Bambara is equally insightful because she
discusses how the revolutionary fervor of the 1960s dissipated and the impact of this on society. She laments that the 1980s was an era of chaos re-
quiring much work. For Bambara the 1980s were a time of personal refocusing for the greater purpose of social transformation. Further she reveals
to Tate the importance of the writer to discern what regular folk and ruling class folk see. This exchange provides extremely important insight into
a major impetus of her work—giving voice to common folk. Her second
novel, *Those Bones Are Not My Child*, a fictional recasting of the horrific Atlanta child murders, follows this motif. Those closest to her at the time were
aware that she was working on this novel and perhaps understood what she
meant about writers voicing perspectives of both common and ruling class
folk.

In addition to this, another important issue broached in the Tate dialogue
was what it means to be female and black and her unique perspective as a
writer because of this. As part of her explanation of the intricacies of these
dynamics she defines herself as a "nationalist and a feminist" whose focus is
empowerment and development of black women. The interview with Tate is
a true gem because Bambara reveals how her interests as a writer emerged,
and how her focus shifted toward film and away from fiction.[22]

Zala Chandler's 1990 interview with Sonia Sanchez and Toni Cade Bambara is as instructive as the Louis Massiah interview, for it also provides important insights into what she believed were her greatest personal, intellectual, and artistic influences. Once again Bambara cites the women from the Harlem community (sanctified churches, trade unions, women's clubs, and the National Negro Congress) as the most influential figures in her life. In explaining this she makes clear the importance of African American folk and folk roots on her work; she cites the tap dancers, bebop "musicians of the forties and fifties," her mother, and Chitlin' Circuit women as the role models who drove the aesthetics and foundations of her fiction.[23] She also claims Beauty Parlor women and Sanctified Women as her first "conscious" heroines'[24] which confirms the prominence of common folk in her fiction.

Throughout the Zala Chandler interview Bambara echoes ideas from previous interviews about merging the political and spiritual to achieve her iteration of "wholeness" that culls numerous aspects of black culture. For example, in this discussion she revisits specific spiritual and political forces that guide her life and her commitment to making these forces work together. Readers familiar with "The Organizers Wife" and *The Salt Eaters* know well her commitment to getting these forces to join hands, much the same way they united during the Civil Rights Movement. Perhaps the most important aspect of the Chandler conversation is the insight Bambara provides about the what and why of her novel *The Salt Eaters*, which she says is about being whole on a "political, psychic, spiritual, cultural, intellectual, aesthetic, physical, and economic level."[25] In addition, this novel is meant to function as one voice; an organized collective response to oppression of people of color. So while each character has a different personal narrative, their collective ailment and goal is what binds them. In fact, this was a primary impetus of all of her work in film, organizing, and writing.

Each is proof, or confirmation of her enduring spirit and legacy. What is unmistakable (in fact it is a dominant theme in *Those Bones*) is the importance of the community and her emphasis on constant critical analysis and the questioning of authority as the safest route to justice and righteous human behavior.[26]

Akasha Hull's conversation with Bambara in 1987 at San Francisco State University is a rich interview because it is one of the few where she intimately discusses her novel *Those Bones Are Not My Child* (at the time of the interview it was tentatively titled "If Blessing Comes" and is referred to in other interviews with variations of this title) as well as her commitment to filmmaking. In their dialogue Bambara makes clear her passion for film. She tells Hull how her last novel is a marriage of fictional impulse, documentary impulse, investigative journalism, and detective mystery genre. She explains it as "a little of this, a little of that—it has been crazy."[27] However, she rejects Hull's attempt to categorize her novel as anything other than a novel. During this exchange she is firm that her novel, despite being the product of "lot of notes [and the] process [being a] blending [of] this and that," is indeed a novel.[28] She goes on to explain to Hull that it was a long journey for the notes she was keeping on the Atlanta child murders to evolve to a fictional form, but that a major function or purpose that her novel performs is to act, to find the truth instead of accepting an "official version" of the truth:

> All I'm asking, essentially, is do we understand what it means when you buy into the official version of things? I mean, we know why we do it because it's easier. To be responsible for your eyes or be responsible for what you hear, what you know, it takes a lot of energy, a lot of courage. In so many ways it seems easier to wait for that phony, bogus, official version, even though you know damn well that it's not being composed in our interest. At least it gives us something to gripe about. . . . I think it's a funny addiction too; the addiction to official versions; to spend life pushing up against 'em and reacting to them. I know many people who are addicted. Can't wait for the official version to come out so they can say [sucks her teeth and turns her head], something.[29]

Essentially Bambara makes clear that her novel represents a different version that contradicts or at least challenges the "official" one regarding the Atlanta child murders. During this conversation Bambara also broaches the importance of three of the characters in her novel: young Sonny who is abducted, his grandmother and family healer, Lovey, and Zala, who is Lovey's daughter and Sonny's mother. However, as the conversation draws to a close she also makes clear that her interest had shifted to film because it offered her a new language, and because she found the writing profession to be isolating.[30]

Those Bones Are Not My Child once again proved her desire and ability to give voice to those rendered silent—the common folk, the poor, the black, the oppressed. While her editor and close friend Toni Morrison cut the original manuscript significantly (which began as research notes in her notebook during the Atlanta murders), Bambara's narrative voice and structure is unfettered. What started as nonfiction became a novel examining the Atlanta child murders through the Spencer family whose eldest son, Sonny, is missing and eventually returns home. (This is significant because none of the forty missing children were found alive.) Bambara lived in Atlanta at the time and was originally gathering information to write nonfiction about the events. This fictional retelling is compelling because Sonny's return home offers hope for truth and resolution where none previously existed. It is a rewind or rememory. Bambara's fictional account of the murders makes extensive use of facts to report the known but unreported truth about crimes from the perspective of the embattled black Atlanta community—ingenious! Her fictional interior version guides readers into the emotions, thoughts, political corruption, racial and class tensions, and frustrations that members of Atlanta's black community endured during this period of terror.[31] Bambara's rendition redirects readers, makes them feel the personal pain suffered by families amid the corruption and cover-up that many felt took place to conceal the true perpetrators of these crimes.

Morrison managed to pair the text down without sacrificing the difficult questions or vision of the book in the process. As Morrison recounts, the task of editing Bambara's massive text was difficult because of its power. "Every time I started [to edit] I would read it . . . [but I had to] look at it with a surgeon's eye, or look at it coldly and be unimpressed, unseduced" (Boyd 92). The final product is one that perhaps only a longtime editor and close friend could have achieved, for Morrison does not impede Bambara's voice and is true to the vision of the novel.

One constant about Bambara, be it in her essays, films, short stories, novels, or these interviews, is that she is an artist with extraordinary ability to convey the full reality of the black community, from the hustlers, old men, and women to the community activists and the preachers. She does it with honesty, the power of love, and an emphasis on the hard work involved in change. These are the attributes that aid her in challenging readers to interrogate assumptions about themselves. Without a doubt her work from her screenplays to her short stories and essays are infused with an uncompromising determination to tell us the truth about ourselves. It is the only way she knew how to tell stories or talk. Toni Morrison offers what is perhaps the best insight into Bambara the person and the artist: "She read the world [. . .]—its symbols, you know, the things behind things" (Boyd 97). Indeed, her fiction aptly conveyed the parent behind the child that became a successful adult, the wife who supports her famous spouse, the brother struggling with fatherhood, the wisdom of women of the night, the folk listening to the speaker on the corner, the lament of parents who have lost a child when there are no answers. And, poet Amiri Baraka's remarks after her death in 1995 are an appropriate summation of Bambara the writer:

Toni was part of the rush of Black women writers that flowed out of the Black Arts sixties, a smoking magma of the real. Who converted the concrete dialectic of our struggle into a complex reflection of people's lives and minds. . . . She gave a living cast to our real life struggles. . . . She wrote of Black people, women, men, children, as workers, mothers, wives, husbands, sons and daughters, revolutionaries, militants, community organizers, nationalists, their families, the participants, the onlookers, bystanders . . . innocent or otherwise. She created a cast of the real people of our world. (Baraka 109)

What is remarkable about Bambara is that she achieved this in all of her work void of superfluity or hyperbole. Indeed, Baraka's words ring true because Bambara always sought to understand the whole of the matter, the "things behind the things." And her impetus for such understanding was transformation and renewal through resistance. The focus of her work really was "a living cast to our real life struggles"; the ubiquitous raison d'etre of her art was "straight up fiction" for the people.

However, it is best to understand Bambara the artist, activist, and person in her own words. During her 1980 interview with Kalamu ya Salaam, "Searching for the Mother Tongue," she explains through the character Fred in her novel *The Salt Eaters* what she deems to be all too common for black folk. She tells ya Salaam, ". . . colored people, Negro people are fours. The thing about fours is that if they invest too much time looking at how they are boxed in on all four sides they never look up and know that they can build upward. To constantly be looking at those four sides is to stay in prison, is to collaborate with your captives, indeed is to lend them energy, which is the same thing as providing them with the power to keep you locked in" (ya Salaam 51). These words characterize Bambara as an artist and person who would never accept constraints; it simply was not an option for her. To effectively hurdle the constraints of language she transmuted her ideas into film. The only option for her was to "try to break past" to develop "a whole new thing" (51). This is why her Black Aesthetic fiction utilizing oral/aural techniques successfully captured the sensibilities of working-class black folk and reflected a multitude of interrelated aesthetics that situated "African cultures in America in various geopolitical contexts" (Bolden 22–23). Whether the issue is racism, sexism, or genre—nothing imprisoned Bambara's life or art.

It is for all these reasons I lament that I never had the opportunity to meet and spend time with Toni Cade Bambara. I can only revel, second hand, in the fond reflections of some of her close friends. Despite this I still feel a deep personal connection to her life and work because her essays, short stories, and fiction have had a profound impact on me as both a black male engaging feminism, and as a father. Over the years I have heard many stories about Bambara from her friends and scholars that knew her well. These stories made me laugh and jealous that I never met her. Secretly I hold out hope that perhaps publishing this important collection of her ideas and words will somehow conjure her up like one of her "other dimension" characters from *The Salt Eaters* or the way young Sonny reappears in *Those Bones Are Not My Child*, so that I might learn one more thing from her. It would also afford me an opportunity to personally thank her for a body of riveting work that brought me and others so much joy and understanding of feminism, of Black Nationalism, of the Black Arts Movement, of black vernacular culture, and of self.

This book is indebted, first and foremost to Toni Cade Bambara, and scholars (such as Guy-Sheftall, Morrison, Butler-Evans, Chandler, Hull, Ikard, ya Salaam, Tate, Bonetti, Traylor, Holmes, and Wall) whose commitment has kept the embers of interest in her art alive. I am also grateful to those individuals that helped, encouraged, and supported me during this project. I wish to thank Tracy Sharpley-Whiting who during one of our many conversations a decade ago suggested Bambara as a research topic; Dana Williams, Jerry Ward, Jr., and Joyce A. Joyce for encouraging me to pursue this book project; Louis Massiah for his graciousness and assistance; Billy for gathering "clean" copies of the interviews; Kay Bonetti and Akasha Hull for their diligence in keeping the record straight; the interviewers and publishers who granted permissions to reprint the selected interviews; Tabitha Smith for her assistance with getting everything together; and Walter Biggins at University Press of Mississippi for his understanding, patience, and persistence to get the manuscript to publication. I am confident that Bambara would be pleased with the collective effort—on myriad levels—involved in the publication of this book of her thoughts and ideas.

TL

Notes

1. In the preface of Bambara's first collection of short stories, *Gorilla, My Love*, she explains that this is the type of fiction that she writes, fiction that does not steal from people's private lives.

2. Kay Bonetti, "An Interview with Toni Cade Bambara," American Audio Prose Library Inc., February 1982.

3. See "A Sort of Preface" in *Gorilla, My Love*. Also this is mentioned in "Toni Cade Bambara: Voices from the Gaps: University of Minnesota," http://voices.cla.umn.edu/artistpages/bambaraToni.php.

4. In *The Black Woman* (1970) Bambara's mother lists her name as Helen Cade Brehon in her essay "Looking Back." In *Savoring the Salt: The Legacy of Toni Cade Bambara*, Linda Janet Holmes and Cheryl A. Wall, eds. (Philadelphia: Temple University Press, 2008) her mother's name is said to be Helen Henderson (Brehon) Cade, and her father is listed as Walter Cade, II. Also see Claudia Tate interview, 1983.

5. See her interview with Louis Massiah. Also similar ground is covered in "Toni Cade Bambara: Voices from the Gaps: University of Minnesota." Also see Claudia Tate interview, 1983.

6. See "Toni Cade Bambara: Voices from the Gaps: University of Minnesota."

7. Ibid., 1.

8. Ibid., 1.

9. Ibid., 1.

10. Ibid., 1–2.

11. Ibid., 1. Also see James D. Hart and Philip Leininger's entry about Bambara in *The Oxford Companion to American Literature*, 1995.

12. Bambara acknowledges the power of writing as an activist vocation during her 1980 interview with Kalamu ya Salaam in *First World*. A few years after the publication of *The Salt Eaters* she relocated to Philadelphia and began to work with film, because she felt it afforded her more room to express herself. She mentions the reason for her shift and the importance of film for her as an effective medium during her 1987 San Francisco State dialogue with Akasha Hull.

13. Bambara makes this point very clearly during her dialogue with Akasha Hull in 1987 at San Francisco State University. She also discusses the writer as new medium notion in ya Salaam and Bonetti interviews.

14. See "Toni Cade Bambara: Voices from the Gaps: University of Minnesota," 2–3.

15. See "Toni Cade Bambara: Voices from the Gaps: University of Minnesota," for the brief discussion of Bambara's belief that film was the best medium for exposing the brutality and inhumanity of the MOVE headquarters bombing, 3.

16. See Akasha Hull interview, 1987. During this discussion she declared film her preferred art form over writing.

17. Ibid.

18. Ibid.

19. Ibid.

20. This is the topic of her interviews with Kay Bonetti and Kalamu ya Salaam. Also, see "Toni Cade Bambara: Voices from the Gaps: University of Minnesota," 3.

21. See Kalamu ya Salaam interview with Bambara, "Searching for the Mother Tongue," *First World* 2, no. 4 (1980): 48–53.

22. See Claudia Tate interview, included in this book, for more about this discussion. Bambara offers very similar analysis during her dialogue with Hull at San Francisco State University in 1987.

23. See "Toni Cade Bambara: Voices from the Gaps: University of Minnesota," 1. She discusses these influences in her Claudia Tate interview.

24. Ibid., 1.

25. See Zala Chandler's interview with Bambara, "Voices Behind the Veil: An Interview with Toni Cade Bambara and Sonia Sanchez," in Joanne M. Braxton and Andrea Nicola McLaughlin, eds., *Wild Women in the Whirlwind*.

26. A major theme of the novel *Those Bones Are Not My Child* is that our duty as citizens, as intelligent members of society is to make everyone accountable—parents, politicians, the police, members of neighborhoods. Such accountability averts the possibility of tragedies like the Atlanta child murders from occurring. This is not to say that Bambara is a negative person, but that she championed a heavy dose of critical inquiry, at every level.

27. In this very candid interview with Akasha Hull, Bambara explains the impetus and method of her novel, which at that time she was calling "If Blessing Comes."

28. Originally she was taking notes to report on the events what were occurring and spent time trying to figure out whether to make it nonfiction or fiction, but settled on fiction. Also it is important to keep in mind that she shifted her focus to filmmaking; the influence is visible in the text.

29. Again, during the interview with Hull Bambara goes on to discuss how eventually the form or shape of the novel presented itself to her; it emerged and announced itself to her. This project stemmed from essays she initially intended to write about the murders that were taking place in Atlanta.

30. In several of her interviews during the 1980s Bambara remarks how film is her passion and that she felt it was the best medium for saying what she wanted to say (interview with Claudia Tate is one example), showing what she envisioned in her mind that words no longer successfully allowed her to do. During her interview with Hull she makes a declaration that she had already shifted in new direction of artistic expression—film.

31. See "Toni Cade Bambara: Voices from the Gaps: University of Minnesota," 3, for the discussion of *Those Bones*, which took Bambara roughly twelve years to write and research.

Works Cited

Bambara, Toni Cade. *Gorilla, My Love*. New York: Random House, 1972; Pocket Books, 1973; Vintage Books, 1981.

———. "On the Issue of Roles." In *The Black Woman: An Anthology*, edited by Toni Cade Bambara, 101–10. New York: New American Library, 1970.

———. *The Salt Eaters*. New York: Random House, 1980; Vintage Books, 1987.

———. "Salvation Is the Issue." In *Black Women Writers (1950–1980): A Critical Evaluation*, edited by Mari Evans, 41–71. Garden City, NY: Anchor/Doubleday, 1984.

———. *Those Bones Are Not My Child*. New York: Random House, 1999.

———. "What It Is I Think I'm Doing Anyhow." In *The Writer on Her Work*, edited by Janet Sternburg, 153–68. New York: W. W. Norton and Company, 1980.

Baraka, Amiri. "Toni." In *Savoring the Salt: The Legacy of Toni Cade Bambara*, edited by Linda Janet Holmes and Cheryl A. Wall, 109–112. Philadelphia: Temple University Press, 2008.

Bolden, Tony. *Afro-Blue: Improvisations in African American Poetry and Culture*. Urbana and Chicago: University of Illinois Press, 2005.

Boyd, Valerie. "'She was just outrageously brilliant': Toni Morrison Remembers Toni Cade Bambara." In *Savoring the Salt: The Legacy of Toni Cade Bambara*, edited by Linda Janet Holmes and Cheryl A. Wall, 88–99. Philadelphia: Temple University Press, 2008.

Curtright, Lauren. "Toni Cade Bambara: Voices from the Gaps: University of Minnesota," http://voices.cla.umn.edu/artistpages/bambaraToni.php.

Guy-Sheftall, Beverly. "Toni Cade Bambara, Black Feminist Foremother." In *Savoring the Salt: The Legacy of Toni Cade Bambara*, edited by Linda Janet Holmes and Cheryl A. Wall, 117–18. Philadelphia: Temple University Press, 2008.

Hart, James, D., and Philip Leininger. "Bambara, Toni Cade." In *The Oxford Companion to American Literature*. Oxford University Press, 1995.

Lewis, Thabiti. "Philadelphia Interview/Conversation with Massiah," June 2003.

Tally, Justine. "Not About to Play It Safe: An Interview with Toni Cade Bambara." *Revista Canaria de Estudios Ingleses*, November 11, 1985.

Tate, Claudia, ed. *Black Women Writers at Work*. New York: Continuum, 1983.

Traylor, Eleanor, W. "Recalling the Black Woman." In *The Black Woman*, edited by Toni Cade Bambara. New York: Washington Square Press, 2005.

ya Salaam, Kalamu. "Searching for the Mother Tongue." *First World*, 2, no. 4 (1980): 48–53.

Chronology

1939	Born Miltona Mirkin Cade (named after her father's employer—Milton Mirkin) on 25 March in New York City to Helen Cade Brehon (sometimes seen as Helen Brent Henderson Cade Brehon) and Walter Cade II. She and her brother, Walter Cade, her only sibling, grow up primarily in New York and New Jersey.
1944 or 1945	Changes her name in Kindergarten to "Toni." Is known as Toni Cade.
1949	Family moves from Harlem.
1953	Attends John Adams High School in Ozone Park in Queens, New York.
1955	Bambara publishes three poems in the John Adams High School publication, *The Clipper*. The three poems are titled "Devil's Advocate," "There'll Come a Day," and "Femme Du Monde."
1959	Graduates from Queens College with a B.A. in theater arts and English. Wins the John Golden Award for writing (at Queens College), as well as the Peter Pauper Press Award in Journalism from the *Long Island Star* for her poem "Dumb Snow." Moves to Greenwich Village after graduation. Bambara's first short story "Sweet Town" is published in *Vendome Magazine*. Marries Tony Batten, a documentary filmmaker who had also attended high school in Queens. They divorce within one year but maintain a friendship. Her second published short story, "Mississippi Ham Rider," appears in the *Massachusetts Review*.
1959–1961	Works as a family and youth caseworker at the New York Department of Welfare and embarks on an M.A. in American literature from City College of New York.
1961	Journeys to Europe to write for a short while.
1961–1962	Works as Director of Recreation in the psychiatric division of Metro Hospital in New York City.

1962–1965   Works as Program Director of the Colony Settlement House while finishing M.A. work.

1965   Completes her M.A. in American literature from City College of New York.

1965–69   Begins teaching in City College's SEEK (Search for Education, Elevation, Knowledge) program for four years, where during this time she is a very influential force. She also worked with its black theater group as well as with publications (*Obsidian*, *Onyx*, and the *Paper*). During this period Bambara becomes involved in numerous sociopolitical issues and community groups.

1968   Begins to work on *The Black Woman* while teaching at City College.

1969   Resigns from City College of New York to accept a position at Livingston College (at Rutgers University) in New Jersey.

1969–1974   Assistant professor at Livingston College, where she is active with black student organizations and arts groups (Malcolm Players, Sisters in Consciousness, and Harambee dancers) for five years, winning a service award.

1970   Adopts the surname Bambara after she discovers it as a signature in a sketchbook found in a trunk of her grandmother's things. Gives birth to only child, Karma Bene Bambara. Karma's father is Gene Lewis, a model, singer, and actor. Edits and contributes to *The Black Woman*, an anthology that makes connections between civil rights and the women's movement and includes fiction, nonfiction, and poetry by well-known writers such as Nikki Giovanni, Alice Walker, and Paule Marshall. An important book, it is a modern innovator in highlighting, as issues of justice, African American women's lives.

1971   Publishes edited book of fiction, *Tales and Stories for Black Folks*, which includes stories from her students. Intended audience is high school and college students, but it proves to have broader appeal.

1972   Publishes her first collection of short stories, *Gorilla, My Love*, and becomes a reviewer for *Liberator Magazine*.

1973   Holds a joint book party with poet Quincy Troupe in New York for her first collection of short stories, *Gorilla, My Love*. Visits Cuba where she meets with women's organizations and women workers who inspire her to think further about the connection between writing and social activism. Spends several days at the Cuban Film Institute watching Cuban films.

1974   Lives on E. 124th Street in Spanish Harlem before she quits Livingston College and leaves New York. Moves with her daughter Karma to Atlanta, seeking connections to spiritual and black southern roots. Purchases 1556 Mayflower Avenue property.

1975   In May Bambara is invited to Vietnam as a guest of the Women's Union of the Democratic Republic of Vietnam. She travels with three other women as part of this delegation. This Federation of Vietnamese Women and her visit moves her more deeply into community organizing and influences some of the stories in her next collection of fiction. In July of 1975 she visits Hanoi for ten days and spends her time there with the Central Bureau of the Women's Union. Visiting professor in Afro-American Studies at Emory University as part of Inter-Institutional program with Atlanta University. Coedits with Leah Wise a special issue of *Southern Exposure*, titled *Southern Black Utterances Today* (vol. 3, no. 1).

1975–1979   Writer in residence at the Neighborhood Arts Center (NAC). Spends part of her time trying to foster networking opportunities for African American writers in the South—this leads to the formation of the Southern Collective of African American Writers.

1976   Visiting Faculty at Stephens College.

1977   Spelman hires Bambara to serve in NEH curriculum program. Helps to develp course, Images of Women in Media.

1977–78   Publishes a second collection of short stories, *The Sea Birds Are Still Alive*, which receives mixed reviews.

1977–1979   Instructor in the School of Social Work at Atlanta University.

1978   Begins work on her first novel, *The Salt Eaters*.

1978–79   Writer-in-residence at Spelman College.

1980   Publishes *The Salt Eaters* to critical acclaim. For a short while, she lives at 991 Simpson Street in Atlanta, Georgia. Bambara assists with the planning of Other Revolution Film Series. She also visits Brazil.

1981   *The Salt Eaters* is issued in paperback and wins the American

	Book Award. Also is awarded the prestigious Langston Hughes Society Award at City College. Bambara receives a National Endowment for the Arts Literature Grant.
1982	*The Salt Eaters* is published in the United Kingdom.
1985	Bambara leaves Atlanta and moves to Philadelphia. Lives in Germantown at 5720 Wissahickon Avenue. Works with Louis Massiah, founder/director of the Scribe Video Center, and improves her film editing skills. She also teaches some filmmaking workshops. Makes her second trip to Cuba with a group of African American women writers headed by Jayne Cortez.
1986	*The Salt Eaters* wins awards from Medallion and the Zora Neale Hurston Society. Bambara works as writer and narrator for Louis Massiah's *The Bombing of Osage Avenue*, which wins the Best Documentary Academy Award and awards from the Pennsylvania Association of Broadcasters and Black Hall of Fame. Narrates, performs, edits, and writes for documentary films such as the *United Hands Community Land Trust's More than Property*, Frances Negron's series on Puerto Rico, Nadine Patterson's documentary on Anna Russell Jones, John Akumfrah's *Seven Songs of Malcolm*, and documentaries on John Coltrane and Cecil B. Moore.
1989	Is honored with citations of merit from Detroit and Atlanta.
1992	*The Salt Eaters* is reprinted by Vintage. Bambara serves as general editor for the African American Life Series of Wayne State University Press and judge for the National Book Awards (fiction).
1993	Bambara is invited to London as a member of the Black Audio Film Collective. She is also invited to participate in Cultural- and Development in Johannesburg, South Africa. Bambara is diagnosed with colon cancer. During the process of recovery, she begins working with Louis Massiah on the documentary, *W. E. B. Du Bois: A Biography in Four Voices*. She is the coordinating writer for Massiah's film. Halie Gerima gives the cash from his Oscar Micheaux Award to Bambara.
1994	Appears in *Midnight Ramble* as part of "The American Experience" public television series that documents early African American cinema. Also attends National Black Arts Festival.
1995	W. E. B. Du Bois film biography is released; has a very posi-

tive reception. Bambara dies of colon cancer on December 9 in Germantown, Pennsylvania, at the age of fifty-six.

1996   *Deep Sightings and Rescue Missions: Fiction, Essays, and Conversations* is published posthumously with the help of Toni Morrison and Bambara's daughter, Karma.

1999   *Those Bones Are Not My Child* is published posthumously.

Conversations
with Toni Cade Bambara

Commitment:
Toni Cade Bambara Speaks

Beverly Guy-Sheftall/1979

From *Sturdy Black Bridges: Visions of Black Women in Literature*, edited by Roseann P. Bell, Bettye J. Parker, and Beverly Guy-Sheftall (Anchor Books, 1979). Reprinted by permission of Beverly Guy-Sheftall.

Sheftall: Would you describe your early life and what caused you to start writing?

Bambara: I can't remember a time when I was not writing. The original motive was to try to do things that we were not encouraged to do in the language arts programs in the schools, namely, to use writing as a tool to get in touch with the self. In the schools, for example, writing, one of the few crafts we're taught, seems to be for the purpose of teaching people how to plagiarize from the dictionary or the encyclopedia and how to create as much distance from your own voice as possible. That was called education. I'd call it alienation. You had to sift out a lot, distort a lot, and lie a lot in order to jam the stuff of your emotional, linguistic, cultural experience into that form called the English composition.

The original motive for writing at home was to give a play to those notions that wouldn't fit the English composition mold, to try and do justice to a point of view, to a sense of self. Later on, I discovered that there was a certain amount of applause that could be gotten if you turned up with the Frederick Douglass play for Negro History Week or the George Washington Carver play for the assembly program. That talent for bailing the English teachers out created stardom, and that became another motive.

As I got older, I began to appreciate the kinds of things you could tap and release and learn about self if you had a chance to get cozy with pencil and paper. And I discovered too that paper is very patient. It will wait on you to come up with whatever it is, as opposed to sitting in class and having to raise your hand immediately in response to someone else's questions, someone else's concerns.

I don't know that I began getting really serious about writing until maybe five years ago. Prior to that, in spite of all good sense, I always thought writing was rather frivolous, that it was something you did because you didn't feel like doing any work. But in the last five or six years I've come to appreciate that it is a perfectly legitimate way to participate in struggle. That writing, sharing insights, keeping a vision alive, is of value and that is pretty much the motive for writing now. Although I can't really say I have a motive for writing now. I'm compelled. I don't think I could stop if I wanted to.

Sheftall: Do you remember the very first story you wrote and the circumstances surrounding it?

Bambara: No, no. I was really little. I'm talking about kindergarten. Sometimes even now, a line will come out that will take me back to some utterance made in a story or poem I wrote or I tried to write when I was in pink pajamas and bunny slippers. It's weird. I've been in training, you might say, for quite a while. Still am.

Sheftall: Were you conditioned by your family members to assume a traditional female role? I'm asking this because of the number of black female children in your fiction who do not conform to American society's notion of what is "proper" female behavior.

Bambara: I think within my household not a great deal of distinction was made between pink and blue. We were expected to be self-sufficient, to be competent, and to be rather nonchalant about expertise in a number of areas. Within the various neighborhoods I've lived in, there was such a variety of expectations regarding womanhood or manhood that it was rather wide-open. In every neighborhood I lived in, for example, there were always big-mouthed women, there were always competent women, there were always beautiful women, independent women as well as dependent women, so that there was a large repertoire from which to select. And it wasn't until I got older, I would say maybe in college, that I began to collide with the concepts and dynamics of "role-appropriate behavior" and so forth. I had no particular notion about being groomed along one particular route as opposed to another as a girl-child. My self-definitions were strongly internal and improvisational.

Sheftall: Take the little girl in "Gorilla, My Love," a favorite story of mine. Would you say that she was like little girls you grew up with? Does she come out of your personal experience?

Bambara: I would say that she's a highly selective fiction. There are certain kinds of spirits that I'm *very* appreciative of, people who are very tough, but very compassionate. You put me in any neighborhood, in any city, and I will tend to gravitate toward that type. The kid in "Gorilla" (the story as well as in that collection) is a kind of person who will survive, and she's triumphant in her survival. Mainly because she's so very human, she cares, her caring is not careless. She certainly is not autobiographical except that there are naturally aspects of my own personality that I very much like that are similar to hers. She's very much like people I like. However, I would be hard pressed to point out her source in real life.

Sheftall: Have women writers influenced you as much as male writers?

Bambara: I have no clear ideas about literary influence. I would say that my mother was a great influence, since mother is usually the first map maker in life. She encouraged me to explore and express. And, too, the fact that people of my household were big on privacy helped. And I would say that people that I ran into helped, and I ran into a great many people because we moved a lot and I was always a nosey kid running up and down the street, getting into everything. Particular kinds of women influenced the work. For example, in every neighborhood I lived in there were always two types of women that somehow pulled me and sort of got their wagons in a circle around me. I call them Miss Naomi and Miss Gladys, although I'm sure they came under various names. The Miss Naomi types were usually barmaids or life-women, nighttime people with lots of clothes in the closet and a very particular philosophy of life, who would give me advice like, "When you meet a man, have a birthday, demand a present that's hockable, and be careful." Stuff like that. Had no idea what they were talking about. Just as well. The Miss Naomis usually gave me a great deal of advice about beautification, how to take care of your health and not get too fat. The Miss Gladyses were usually the type that hung out the window in Apartment 1-A leaning on the pillow giving single-action advice on numbers or giving you advice about how to get your homework done or telling you to stay away from those cruising cars that moved through the neighborhood patrolling little girls. I would say that those two types of women, as well as the women who hung out in the beauty parlors (and the beauty parlors in those days were perhaps the only womanhood institutes we had—it was there in the beauty parlors that young girls came of age and developed some sense of sexual standards and some sense of what it means to be a woman growing up)—it was those women who had the most influence on the writing.

I think that most of my work tends to come off the street rather than from other books. Which is not to say I haven't learned a lot as an avid reader. I devour pulp and print. And of course I'm part of the tradition. That is to say, it is quite apparent to the reader that I appreciate Langston Hughes, Zora Hurston, and am a product of the sixties spirit. But I'd be hard pressed to discuss literary influences in any kind of intelligent way.

Sheftall: Did you grow up in New York primarily?
Bambara: Primarily.

Sheftall: Let's move to some of your reactions to the literary scene. What would you consider to be some contemporary or past positive images of black women in literature, either by male or female or black or white writers?
Bambara: I would define "positive" as usable, characters who can teach us valuable lessons of life, characters who are rounded and who give dimension to the type or stereotype that they are closest to. For example, Sula in the Morrison novel is interesting. She's a champion. She's an adventurer, and she gives us another dimension of the bitch stereotype. She makes us aware of how many people are locked up in that particular cage. Eva, who very much resembles the stereotypic matriarch, is more than that and she too helps to break open that old stereotype and force us to look for qualities, lessons, eclipsed by the stereotypic label. I regard them as positive, for they touch deep. In the contemporary poetry—that is, the poetry that came out of the Neo-Black Arts Movement—there are female personae who are assertive and rounded and they also break open the bitch stereotype for us, so that we find under that label locked-up vibrancy—activities, combatants, the Harriet Tubman heirs, people who come from that championship tradition. That's what I would call positive and in fact there are very few works that are available to us now, say in the last decade, that are not like that. We have very little deadwood in the works that have come out of the sixties and are currently being produced. Very few flat, stupid, useless, and careless portraits.

Sheftall: Is there a particular black woman writer of fiction who you think best illuminates the black female experience, specifically the double oppression of race and sex?

Bambara: No, and I think that's okay. I think if we were designing a course that attempted to project the profile of the contemporary black woman, particularly in respect to double or triple oppression, to someone who did not understand it, it would be necessary to pull out a lot of people because there are a lot of experiences. There is no *the* woman or *the* experience or *the* profile. I would assemble the works of writers like Zora Hurston, Toni Morrison, Carolyn Rodgers, Lucille Clifton, Eloise Lofton, and a good many others and particularly young writers who are coming out of the workshops, in the Southeast particularly, and out of the Berkeley group.

Sheftall: Do you think the black woman writer has been treated fairly by the critical community, both black and white?

Bambara: I have no idea. It's not something I have any comments on because it's not something I generally think about, that is to say, the black woman writer. We know for sure that any cultural product of black people has not been treated intelligently and usefully by white critics. That's one kind of answer. The fact that a good many black women writers do not get into anthologies that are put together by black men is another kind of answer. The fact that black women critics sometimes approach black women's writing as though they were highly particular and had no connection to the group traditions, that's another kind of issue.

I'm not so much concerned with whether black women writers are dealt with fairly but rather with what they're dealing with. And I think the great accomplishment of particularly the poets of the Neo-Black Arts Movement (sister poets) and perhaps to a lesser degree the dramatists, novelists, short story writers, have contributed a great deal toward not only commenting on, correcting, and countering the stereotypic images, but in blasting open a new road, if you will, for younger writers who are coming along now: dealing with women who have not been dealt with before, raising issues that have not been tackled before, grabbing hold of a vision that we have let slip and maybe never have laid out in print before. The production itself I find far more interesting than critical response.

Sheftall: Near the end of her introduction to *Black-Eyed Susans*, a collection of short stories by and about black women, Mary Helen Washington asserts with respect to the black woman writer that "there still remains something of a sacred-cow attitude in regard to black women that prevents exploration of many aspects of their lives." "There has been a desire," she goes on to say, "to protect and revere the black woman's image." She argues then that we need books about black women who have nervous breakdowns, who are "overwhelmed by sex," who are not faithful, who abuse and neglect their children, and so forth. That is, we also need stories about "real black women," stories which "interpret the entire range and spectrum of the experiences of black women." Would you agree with her assessment of the black woman writer with respect to these issues?

Bambara: I don't approach literature from quite that direction. I think I understand what she's saying, but writing for me is still an act of language first and foremost. I don't know that I need to read a book about a nervous breakdown in order to understand nervous breakdowns or to protect my health. As an act of language, literature is a spirit informer—an energizer. A lot of energy is exchanged in the reading and writing of books and that gets into the debate of whether it is more important to offer a usable truth or to try to document the many truths or realisms that make up the black woman's experience.

I think I see her point and it's all very lovely but it doesn't concern me, and I'm not altogether sure it's valid or true. It is true that we're so defensive about our detractors, which I think is what one of her points is, that we are not approaching the complexity of ourselves in a fearless way. That is true, but I don't know that the nervous breakdown is what I would argue for. I would argue rather that there is an aspect of black spirit, of inherent black nature, that we have not addressed: the tension, the power that is still latent, still colonized, still frozen and untapped, in some 27 million black people. We do not know how to unleash, we do not even know how to speak of it in a courageous manner, *yet. I* think that is because we have been so long on the defensive and have invested a great deal of time and energy posturing and trying to prove that indeed we are as clean as they are. Since the sixties, however, a great many of us have been released from that posturing through having dialogues with each other which is a very radical and new dimension to the dialogue of cultural worker and community. It is in relation to potential that I might argue Mary Helen's same general point. Namely, that we are not terribly fearless and courageous and thoroughgoing in dealing with the complexity of the black experience, the black spirit. As a matter of fact, music is probably the only mode we have used to speak of that complexity. But I would argue the point in relation to other aspects of self rather than to nervous breakdowns and the kinds of things that Mary Helen is talking about, which is not to say that it has no usefulness, but it doesn't strike me as a priority at all.

Sheftall: Do you think that the black woman has an advantage or special perspective that may enable her to reveal those aspects of the black experience or black spirit to which you refer?

Bambara: No, I wouldn't say that black women or children or elders or men or any other sector of the community are any more in command of it or in touch with it than any other. I find it interesting in this period, the seventies, that we have begun to embrace within our community (and we can see parallels in the national as well as international community) an interest in holistic healing systems: astrology, voodoo, TM, etc. No, I don't think that any group within the community has any monopoly on that kind of wisdom, a grasp on that new way to prepare for the future.

Sheftall: Speaking of parallels, have your travels revealed to you how American black and other Third World women can link up in their struggles to liberate themselves from the various kinds of oppression they face as a result of their sexual identity?

Bambara: Yes, I would say that two particular places I visited yielded up a lot of lessons along those lines. I was in Cuba in 1973 and had the occasion not only to meet with the Federation of Cuban Women but sisters in the factories, on the land, in the street, in the parks, in lines, or whatever, and the fact that they were able to resolve a great many class conflicts as well as color conflicts and organize a mass organization says a great deal about the possibilities here. I was in Vietnam in the summer of 1975 as a guest of the Women's Union and again was very much struck by the women's ability to break through traditional roles, traditional expectations, reactionary agenda for women, and come together again in a mass organization that is programmatic and takes on a great deal of responsibility for the running of the nation.

We missed a moment in the early sixties. We missed two things. One, at a time when we were beginning to lay the foundations for a national black women's union and for a national strategy for organizing, we did not have enough heart nor a solid enough analysis that would equip us to respond in a positive and constructive way to the fear in the community from black men as well as others who said that women organizing as women is divisive. We did not respond to that in a courageous and principled way. We fell back. The other moment that we missed was that we had an opportunity to hook up with Puerto Rican women and Chicano women who shared not only a common condition but also I think a common vision about the future and we missed that moment because of the language trap. When people talked about multicultural or multiethnic organizing, a lot of us translated that to mean white folks and backed off. I think that was an error. We should have known what was meant by multicultural. Namely, people of color. Afro-American, Afro-Hispanic, Indo-Hispanic, Asian-Hispanic, and so forth. Not that those errors necessarily doom us. Errors may result in lessons learned. I think we have the opportunity again in this last quarter of the twentieth century to begin forging those critical ties with other communities. It will be done. That is a certainty.

Sheftall: Do you consider it a dilemma for the black woman today who considers herself both a feminist and a warrior in the race struggle?

Bambara: A dilemma? Personally, no. I'm not aware of what the problem is for people who do feel that's a dilemma. I don't know what they're thinking because it's not as if you're a black *or* a woman. I don't find any basic contradiction or any tension between being a feminist, being a pan-Africanist, being a black nationalist, being an internationalist, being a socialist, and being a woman in North America. I'm not sensitive enough to people caught in the "contradiction" to be able to unravel the dilemma and adequately speak to the question at this particular point in time. My head is somewhere else.

Sheftall: Turning to your own writings, you said in your preface to *The Black Woman*, an anthology of readings by contemporary black women published in 1970, that among other evils this country "regards its women as its monsters." Have you seen over the past seven years or so any changes in this country's attitude toward women, especially the black ones?

Bambara: The country at large, no. You look at *That's My Mama* and I think it's clear that television program really centers around the son and the activities in the barbershop. That's the most dynamic aspect of that drama. But because the mammy looms so large in the American mentality, is such a durable, persistent psychosexual obsession on the part of white people, male and female, that need demands the presence of the mama figure: on the one hand, a gracious, giving, enduring mammy, but also a Hattie McDaniel sass. Sass as a comic-menace element. The menace element is a white fiction that is meshed into our women, that has to do with their whole "momism" pathology. So they get their thing off in three ways through her: She's useful to keep the "boy" thing going; she's the mother's milk nurturer; plus the "hate mom" white thing can be projected onto her.

I don't know that I have seen any change, by and large, in white America. In terms of black America, there are authors still—I'm thinking of John A. Williams in particular, as well as many other writers who don't come to mind at the moment—who are still a little scary in terms of the assertive black woman, still look at Sapphire as a threat, and who do not come to grips with how that myth functions in American society. The bitch helps to justify, for example, hustlers and other collaborators. The presence of the bitch myth also helps those societal restraints that operate on black women, as well as the rest of the community. No, I haven't noticed a lot of change among black male writers either. Ron Milner's women are a change, though.

Sheftall: If you were to do another anthology of readings by contemporary black women today, what kind of pieces would you include?

Bambara: The papers that I was most concerned with at that time never got into the book, and those were position papers from the Women's Caucus of SNCC, of the Panthers, of a number of other organizations that eventually did produce papers, for publication through Third World Women's Alliance. I was particularly concerned with the evolution of women's groups that had begun as consumer education or single-issue action groups, began studying together and engaging in community organizing and are now, some ten years later, the core network of what will soon become, we hope, a national black women's union. I would include in a new collection writings from the campus forces, the prison forces, tenant's groups, and most especially southern rural women's works, particularly from the migrant workers and sharecroppers of the Deep South.

Sheftall: How did you go about selecting the pieces that were included in the collection you edited entitled *Tales and Stories for Black Folks*, which was published in 1972?

Bambara: The first half of the book consists of stories I wished I had read growing up, stories by Alice Walker, Pearl Crayton, and particularly Langston Hughes. The stories in the second half of the book were documents that came out of a course that I was teaching (a freshman composition course, which has always been my favorite). The students had begun working with kids in an independent community school and I asked them to produce term paper projects that were usable to someone. So a great many of them took traditional European tales and changed them so as to promote critical thinking, critical reading for the young people they were working with outside of the class. And out of that group of term papers came a number of really remarkable, thoughtful pieces, such as "The True Story of Chicken Licken," which raises questions about the nature of truth or the nature of responsible journalism. The story pivoted on the idea that perhaps it was not a piece of sky that fell on Chicken Licken's head after all but maybe she got caught up in a community action and got hit on the head by the cops and then they put out a press release that she had been attacked by a piece of cloud. All of the stories in the second half of the book came out of the materials that had been submitted to me by students that year.

Sheftall: You are one of the few black literary artists who could be considered a short story writer primarily. Is this a deliberate choice on your part or coincidental?

Bambara: It's deliberate, coincidental, accidental, and regretful! Regretful, commercially. That is to say, it is financially stupid to be a short story writer and to spend two years putting together eight or ten stories and receiving maybe half the amount of money you would had you taken one of those short stories and produced a novel. The publishing companies, reviewers, critics, are all geared to promoting and pushing the novel rather than any other form.

I prefer the short story genre because it's quick, it makes a modest appeal for attention, it can creep up on you on your blind side. The reader comes to the short story with a mind-set different than that with which he approaches the big book, and a different set of controls operating, which is why I think the short story is far more effective in terms of teaching us lessons.

Temperamentally, I move toward the short story because I'm a sprinter rather than a long-distance runner. I cannot sustain characters over a long period of time. Walking around, frying eggs, being a mother, shopping—I cannot have those characters living in my house with me for more than a couple of weeks. In terms of craft, I don't have the kinds of skills *yet* that it takes to stay with a large panorama of folks and issues and landscapes, and moods. That requires a set of skills that I don't know anything about yet, but I'm learning.

I prefer the short story as a reader, as well, because it does what it does in a hurry. For the writer and the reader make instructive demands in terms of language precision. It deals with economy, gets it said, and gets out of the way. As a teacher, I also prefer the short story for all the reasons given. And yes, I consider myself primarily a short story writer.

Sheftall: You are attempting a novel, though, for the first time?
Bambara: No, not for the first time. Like every other writer, I have fifteen thousand unfinished novels brewing under the bed. But having come to grips with the nature of publishing, I understand that it is shrewd and in my interest to produce a novel before I come out with another collection of short stories, so I'm doing both.

Sheftall: Will the novel be anything like your short stories?
Bambara: Surely, it's the same mind working, after all. They're the same in the sense that the vision hasn't changed. My affinity for certain kinds of people is the same.

Sheftall: Is the setting North or South?
Bambara: It seems to be South. It seems to be everywhere. I've got a sixty-page chunk of it and there are several thousand characters running around and it seems to be vaguely Louisiana and there's also a character who's obviously from New York and there's somebody else who's obviously from the Coast and I have a couple of West Indian folk and I have an Arapaho in there as well as an Aleutian and two people from the Philippines. So I'm not sure what the setting of the novel is. But it's driving me crazy.

Sheftall: That leads me into the next question which is about the process involved in your writing a story. Do you have the whole idea of it before sitting down to write, or does it unfold as you're writing?
Bambara: It depends on how much time you have. There are periods in my life when I know that I will not be able to get to the desk until summer, until months later, in which case I walk around composing while washing dishes and may jot down little definitive notes on pieces of paper which I stick under the phone, in the mirror, and all over the house. At other times, a story mobilizes itself around a single line you've heard that resonates. There's a truth there, something usable. Sometimes a story revolves around a character that I'm interested in. For example, "The Organizer's Wife" in the new collection. I've always been very curious about silent people because most people I know are like myself—very big-mouthed, verbally energetic, and generally clear as to what they're about because their *mouth* is always announcing what they're doing. That story came out of a curiosity. What do I know about people like that? Could I delve into her? The story took shape around that effort.

There are other times when a story is absolutely clear in the head. All of it may not be clear—who's going to say what and where it's taking place or what year it is—but the story frequently comes together at one moment in the head. At other times, stories, like any other kind of writing, and certainly anybody who's writing anything—freshman compositions, press releases, or whatever—has experienced this, that frequently writing is an act of discovery. Writing is very much like dreaming, in that sense. When you dream, you dialogue with aspects of yourself that normally are not with you in the daytime and you discover that you know a great deal more than you thought you did. So there are various kinds of ways that writing comes.

Then, too, there is a kind of—some people call it automatic writing—I call it inspiration. There are times when you have to put aside what you intended to write, what got you to the desk in the first place, and just go with the story that is coming out of you, which may or may not have anything to do with what you planned at all. In fact, a lot of stories (I haven't published any of these because I'm not sure they are mine) and poems have come out on the page that I know do not belong to me. They do not have my sense of vision, my sense of language, my sense of reality, but they're complete. Each of us has experienced this in various ways, in church, or fasting, or in some other kind of state, times when we are available to intelligences that we are not particularly prone to acknowledge, given our Western scientific training, which have filled us with so much fear that we cannot make ourselves available to other channels of information. I think most of us have experienced, though we don't talk about it very much, an inspiration, that is to say, an in-breathing that then becomes "enthusiasm," a possession, a living-with, an informing spirit. So some stories come off like that.

Sheftall: Do you make many revisions before the story is finished and ready for publication?

Bambara: Oh yes. I edit mercilessly. Generally, my editing takes the form of cutting. Very frequently, a story will try to get away from me and become a novel. I don't have the staying power for a novel, so when I find it getting to be about thirty or forty pages I immediately start cutting back to six. To my mind, the six-page short story is the gem. If it takes more than six pages to say it, something is the matter. So I'm not too pleased in that respect with the new collection, *The Sea Birds Are Still Alive*. Most of those stories are too sprawling and hairy for my taste, although I'm very pleased, feel perfectly fine about them as pieces. But as stories, they're too damn long and dense.

Sheftall: Let's move to a specific discussion of *The Sea Birds*, your most recently published collection of short stories, which I thoroughly enjoyed. Barbara Mahone, in her review which appears in the May/June 1977 issue of *First World*, asserts that your handling of black male-female relationships is different from at least two other black female writers, Alice Walker and Nto-zake Shange, because they leave, she says, "this bitter residue of bad feelings between men and women," whereas in your stories, "the net social effect" is more positive. Do you agree with her?

Bambara: One might just as easily argue that the difference is that they're telling the truth and I'm not. Or one could just as easily argue that they're getting into the more painful side of the relationship and I am not. Tempera-mentally, I'm much more concerned with the caring that lies beneath the antagonisms between black men and black women. There is a great deal of static that informs our relationships, above and beyond the political wedge that has been jammed between us by myth makers of the oppressor class. Whereas other writers, other women, other people, are more concerned with the hurt of it all, the hurt doesn't teach me anything and I'm concerned primarily with usable lessons. The caring does teach me something and I think I can offer a usable something for someone else.

It is very facile to talk about male-female antagonisms in the Western world or in the United States in a pat fashion that enables you to sound as though you're talking about all people. It's easy to talk about *the* War Be-tween the Sexes which is characteristic of the United States as it is no other place. When foreigners watch Hollywood movies and see Clark Gable drop Claudette Colbert in the mud, the response is a gasp. That is something pe-culiarly American, that belligerency, that warfare. A great many folk are in the process of speaking about women/men relationships in our community in that kind of generalized way of trying to make it "universal." That's very dangerous and kind of sloppy and not very valid because what distinguishes relationships between men and women in our community is the level of car-ing that informs the tension.

If a white woman attacks a white man in general or in particular about being a chauvinist pig, underneath that is the legacy of Europe, is the notion of a God complex with the woman as martyr who will forgive everything and manipulate shrewdly under the table with cunning and craft, but mostly she will be a martyr on the cross and that gives her moral superiority to con-demn all or forgive all—to play God. Black women, on the other hand, do not deal with themselves as God, nor do they remove Him from the human frame of reference. We start with the premise "I am not God" and therefore have a right to call you on that play. That's a very different mind-set and a very different frame of reference, a very different moral code. I hope we can get to the point where we recognize, again, that if we love each other, we are concerned with development. And that means being mutually responsible to each other—criticism, hardheaded demands.

Getting back to Barbara Mahone's comment, it's not terribly useful for *me* to make comparisons. One could take her contrast to prove any number of things. I am simply more interested in the caring network that exists between men and women, men and men, women and women, children and elders. One of the reasons those links are links of vulnerability at one moment has to do with the level of caring and the degree to which that caring can push against the synthetic conflicts that white society orchestrates in its interests, not ours.

Sheftall: Of the reviews I've read of *The Sea Birds*, none has mentioned "The Girl's Story," a fascinating though possibly perplexing piece. Why has her family mistaken her first menstrual period for an abortion?
Bambara: Well, this is a family where not much touching goes on, as is played on throughout the story. There are great distances, even though the people live close-quartered. For example, the girl hears a certain quality in her brother's voice only once in a while. She can embrace her grandmother or her grandmother can embrace her only in a very particular kind of way and it's not closeness. It's not touching. In a household like that, it stands to reason that a lot of secretiveness and isolation travel under the guise of privacy. So it's not unlikely at all that they would not know she's begun her menses.

In almost every household that I can think of when I was growing up, the onset of the menstrual period was mysterious and frightening and totally without information and totally without support from the immediate household. Most frequently, young girls could find a sympathetic godmother or maybe some older girl in the neighborhood who understood and recognized it right away and got the wagons in a circle. I know very few households when I was growing up where it would have been dealt with in any other way than it is depicted in the story—which is why the title is general, "A Girl's Story."

Sheftall: Yes, that was an aspect of the story that I suspect many women of past generations can relate to. It is true that many aspects of the menstrual period were and possibly still are shrouded in mystery. What's interesting, however, is that when I have used fiction that mentions this issue with students in my college classes (such as *Browngirl, Brownstones, The Bluest Eye*), many of them have not been very responsive. They tend to think that dealing with circumstances surrounding the first menstrual period in a work of literature is unnecessary and you find yourself saying to them that for some women the experience was traumatic. Some students even found it difficult to remember what it was like.

Bambara: It might be true that the particular traumas and dangers of womanhood are not valued as a crucial part of our culture. As a matter of fact, that is why the cult of the Amazon, the cult of strength, the bear-up-under-everything woman figure came into play because we did not admit, were not allowed to, could not afford to *admit* pain and suffering and hardship. You're not supposed to do that if you're a black woman. In line with that, anyone who's ever visited the neighborhood chiropractor's office or who has ever watched healing services in our own community is probably well aware that black women have tremendous problems with their backs. And I wonder if part of that isn't the unnecessary burden of taking on that cult of strength, that Amazon figure, and internalizing that whole madness.

For students in the generation behind us not to be able to identify with the trauma of the first menses is open to a number of interpretations. I would like to think that their nonchalance or impatient response means that it was all very breezy and pleasant.

The initiation or rites of passage of the young girl is not one of the darlings of American literature. The coming of age for the young boy is certainly much more the classic case. I wonder if it all means that we don't put a value on our process of womanhood.

Sheftall: Have you been generally pleased with the reviews of *Sea Birds*?
Bambara: All of the reviews have been very favorable. Some have been quite cogent and favorable. Some have been stupid and favorable. I found the *First World* review that was in the Chicago *Tribune* by Bruce Allen critically constructive. It focused on the flaws and the faults of the book and I found it very helpful. The piece that Ruby Dee wrote (I'm not sure where it will appear; I imagine in the *Amsterdam News*) I found the most *moving* in the sense that she makes highly particular the public and personal values. It just had me in tears. It helped me to answer some of the questions one always has in one's mind while writing: whether it works, what doesn't work, to what degree is it overdone, to what degree is it too understated, questions of that sort. The Ruby Dee piece was somp'n, honey.

Sheftall: One of the characteristics of your fiction which is apparent in *Gorilla, My Love*, an older collection of short stories, as well as in *The Sea Birds* is the extent to which—though one knows you're there—you can remove yourself from the narrative voice. You don't intrude. Is that deliberate?

Bambara: Well, I'm frequently there. You see, one of the reasons that it seems that the author is not there has to do with language. It has to do with the whole tradition of dialect. In the old days, writers might have their characters talking dialect or slang but the narrator, that is to say, the author, maintained a distance and a "superiority" by speaking a more premiumed language. I tend to speak on the same level as my characters, so it seems as though I am not there, because, possibly, you're looking for another voice.

Sheftall: I rarely get the impression that your fiction comes directly out of your personal experience, even though it's obvious that what you have written about has been filtered through your consciousness. I don't have the impression that these particular characters or that particular incident are very close to what you may have actually experienced. Is that correct?

Bambara: Yes, that's correct. I think it's very rude to write autobiographically, unless you label it autobiography. And I think it's very rude to use friends and relatives as though they were occasions for getting your whole thing off. It's not making your mama a still life. And it's very abusive to your developing craft, to your own growth, not to convert and transform what has come to you in one way into another way. The more you convert the more you grow, it seems to me. Through conversion we recognize again the basic oneness, the connections, or as some blood coined it: "Everything is Everything." So, it's kind of *lazy* (I think that's the better word) to simply record. Also, it's terribly boring to the reader frequently, and, too, it's dodgy. You can't tell to what extent things are fascinating to you because they're yours and to what extent they're useful, unless you do some conversion.

Sheftall: What can we expect from you in the future?

Bambara: I'm working on several things—some children's books, a new collection of short stories, a novel, some film scripts.

"Children of Struggle" is a series I've been working on that dramatizes the role children and youth have played in the struggle for liberation—children of the Underground Railroad, children of Frelimo, children of the Long March, of Granma, of El Grito de Lares, The Trail of Tears, and so forth.

The major question that corners me at the moment is what constitutes development for the systematically underdeveloped. I've tackled the question in several forms. I'm thinking now of putting together a critique of pedagogical perspectives, examining the premises of Freud, Montessori, Piaget, learning theories, educational models, to reveal how the training of children is being approached as a management problem rather than a *development* question; two, that there really are few sound development theories at all. First, we're children to the Freudians, then we're neurotic. No model of adulthood or maturity there. Or, we're innocent babes to be protected from controversy, problems, disturbances; then we're responsible adults, somehow; then we're senile, useless crones. Fanon and of course Friere (*Pedagogy of the Oppressed*) offer another view of the process. But they are too incomplete.

I'm doing a film script about a particular group of combatants in the 1850s (Tubman, Douglass, John Brown, etc.) with the focus on the much neglected figure of Mammy Pleasant, who bankrolled so many of the Kansas actions and set up an intelligence network on the Coast. Fascinating woman!

The new collection begins where *Sea Birds* leaves us, stories that dramatize the international operation of colonialism and celebrates too the international nature of liberation struggles. One is set in Ponce and Mayagüez, Puerto Rico, another in the New Hebrides, another in Laos, another in the Kenyan countryside. I hope to get to Brazil this year and back to Africa as well.

As for the novel—it's still a mystery to me. I started out with a simple story of a carnival society that decides to stage an old slave insurrection as their contribution to the pageant. It's developed into—well, you can imagine. Hard work, writing. A continual act of discovery!

Searching for the Mother Tongue

Kalamu ya Salaam/1980

From *First World* 2, no. 4 (1980). Reprinted by permission of Kalamu ya Salaam.

First World: Are you consciously trying to do anything in particular with your style of writing?

Toni Cade Bambara: I'm trying to learn how to write! I think there have been a lot of things going on in the Black experience for which there are no terms, certainly not in English at this moment. There are a lot of aspects of consciousness for which there is no vocabulary, no structure in the English language which would allow people to validate that experience through the language. I'm trying to find a way to do that.

FW: Do you see yourself, then, essentially in search of a language?

TCB: That's one of the things I'm trying to do.

FW: Why hasn't this happened before? Do you think other writers have tried to do this and been unsuccessful?

TCB: I don't know. I do know that the English language that grew from the European languages has been systematically stripped of the kinds of structures and the kinds of vocabularies that allow people to plug into other kinds of intelligences. That's no secret. That's part of their whole history, wherein people cannot be a higher sovereign than the state. At the time when wise folk were put to the rack was also a time when books were burned, temples razed to the ground, and certain types of language "mysteries"—for lack of a better word—were suppressed. That's the legacy of the West.

I'm just trying to tell the truth and I think in order to do that we will have to invent, in addition to new forms, new modes and new idioms. I think we will have to connect language in that kind of way. I don't know yet what that is.

FW: Do you see any models or any path breakers?

TCB: I think most poets play with that. I think musicians are far more successful with their language. It's become an obsession with me now. I'm trying to break words open and get at the bones, deal with symbols as though they were atoms. I'm trying to find out not only how a word gains its meaning, but how a word gains its power.

FW: Do you see a difference between writers trying to deal with their craft, with words which are part of their craft, and your attempt, and the attempt of other writers, to create a written language in English that can express the African American experience? Is it simply a technical question dealing with craft or . . . ?

TCB: No, I don't think it's a technical question. It's beyond a technical question. I don't know what the term is for that kind of exploration, that kind of obsession, that kind of quest.

FW: Have you seen any examples of this in other writers of the Third World, particularly the decolonialized Third World?

TCB: Yes.

FW: Could you give some examples?

TCB: Amos Tutuola, for example, for the kinds of areas he is exploring, has to invent, has to mediate between whatever language is characteristic of the way he moves in the universe and that other language, the colonial language. That's true of anybody dealing in a language other than their mother tongue, obviously.

FW: Strictly from the African American experience, in your opinion what language would be our mother tongue?

TCB: The language of Langston Hughes, the language of Grandma, the language of "mama say." Mama say don't let cha mouth get you into what, *etc. etc.*

FW: What problems have you had with publishers and editors in getting them to accept this search for a new language. With *The Salt Eaters*, were there any problems with . . . ?

TCB: No, the problems are with me in terms of my own editing. When I edit, I have to decide whether I'm editing for readability or am I editing for that questing. Sometimes I have to compromise or play games . . .

FW: What does that mean?

TCB: Sometimes it's necessary to edit for readability, in which case I have to let go.

FW: In other words, to maintain a bridge to the audience you have to pull back a bit?

TCB: Yeah.

FW: But you didn't have any problems with the editors or publishers?

TCB: No. Well, they raise the usual kind of copy editing questions such as, "Do you mean to drop the 'g' off of doing; is this a typo or is it an expression characteristic of your community; is this a 'coined' phrase or does it have currency?"

FW: Which is interesting because usually when they say "coined phrase" they mean it's counterfeit, whereas if it has current usage or it's commonly in use they say it has currency.

TCB: Yeah. Like the word "artifice"; to make art is to be phony.

FW: When you were doing *The Salt Eaters*, in the process of actually writing it, did you at any time consider yourself in a state of altered consciousness?

TCB: I think that when I write at any time I'm in a state of altered consciousness in the sense that I am self-remembering, that is, I'm acutely aware of a dialogue that is going on between me and the characters which are conjured. I am acutely aware of myself as a reader. I actually am aware of the relationship between what's going on in my head and what I can do with my hands, and that is not the state that I normally walk around and fry the eggs in.

FW: How do you prepare yourself for that?

TCB: Sit down and be still. Unplug the phone and be quiet.

FW: Do you do any type of research for your fiction?

TCB: Not in any conscious, deliberate sort of way, but I'm reading all the time, talking to people all the time, and traveling a lot. I jot down notes. Sometimes I will pursue . . . for example, the original manuscript of *The Salt Eaters* was a short story about a Mardi Gras society that elects to reenact an old slave insurrection in a town experiencing orchestrated conflicts. Some of the characters began speaking Portuguese; I don't speak Portuguese. I had originally set it in some place like New Orleans, or kind of like Galveston (Texas), and the scene shifted, so I went with it and wrote it out. I then found I needed to verify what this was. In about three months I began to do a lot of reading on Palmares and felt that maybe that was where that story was going to take place except I don't have any . . . (interrupting herself) there are no words. I was going to say "control," but that presupposes I was trying to get control and I don't, so that's not the word, but, get a "handle" on it, that the best way to say it. Sometimes, I will do that kind of research. As a rule, I don't do a lot of research.

There's a scene in *The Salt Eaters* where Nilda, the sister of the corn, was thinking about Barnwell and about the jackrabbits—contaminated, radioactive and glowing in the dark. I thought that this was a good metaphor and a nice image but I seriously doubted if radioactive animals glow. So, I had to look that up and found that they didn't. But I like the image, so I figured, well, I'm just going to go ahead and keep it.

This thing I'm working on now requires a great deal of research. I'm trying to put together a Harper's Ferry script. I've never been satisfied with the movies, particularly Hollywood versions . . .

FW: That reference you have to Harper's Ferry in *The Salt Eaters*—does that have anything to do with this project?

TCB: Yes. That's to remind myself of what I'm doing next. I've had a hunch for a long time that Mama Pleasant and Marie Laveau . . . In addition to the work they did that we do know of I have a feeling that they had put together an intelligence network and were very much into the underground railroad. Nobody has documented that yet. I keep waiting and throwing it out there, hoping that someone will go and do the research. I'm researching that now and that requires a lot of time.

I'm not a good researcher. I'm a good research teacher because I'm a detective and I'm nosey. I'm willing to go anywhere to get the information. But I'm not a trustworthy researcher because I reconstruct and most reconstructing means fictionalizing.

FW: Fictionalizing in the sense that you use the basic events to create a new or future scenario?

TCB: More than that. I lie. I make jump cuts, absolute leaps.

FW: Does that have anything to do with your interest in film?

TCB: Yeah, but I didn't mean to say "jump cut," I meant to say quantum leaps. For example, with Mama Pleasant, she had a girl, a laundry worker, who pops up in a couple of other people's diaries as being retarded. Yet, Mama Pleasant used to send her far afield. She was in Lawrence, Kansas, at one time, and she was in another place in Kansas. Around that time John Brown's raids broke out. I have the feeling that Mama Pleasant bankrolled John Brown's raids. So, on my research, I am looking just for the one thing to confirm this so I can forget about it and go and do my work. That's not research.

FW: Actually, you're looking for something to validate a conclusion you have already made rather than just gathering information.
TCB: Right.

FW: Ideally, what would you like *The Salt Eaters* to accomplish?
TCB: Based on the kind of feedback that I've gotten from letters and phone calls, more than the reviews—only since Jerry (Ward) and a few others have started writing have "folk" been giving me some critical feedback; the reviewers in *Newsweek* and *Time* and the *New Yorker* have not been particularly intelligent or informed—but the feedback I've gotten from writers, I wouldn't say younger writers but rather up-and-coming writers, is that *The Salt Eaters* breaks new ground. For people who live with a comfortable molding of the physical and the metaphysical but don't know how to talk about it yet, and don't know whether they have to find a metaphor for talking about spirit, vibes, for talking about what people call psychic phenomenon or whatever, they have called up to say, "Hey, you handled it in a kind of nonchalant way. I feel better. I'll just go ahead and do it."

The other thing, I think is more important, is that there are three kinds of calls I'm making in *The Salt Eaters* through the three institutions in Claybourne that are governed by black people. In the Academy of the Seven Arts, Obie is attempting to bridge the gap between our medicine people and our warriors, and that's a call. I don't think it's terribly important whether I got it nailed in the book. I explore it, I bring it up, but I don't have anywhere to put it or push it. But I think, if it's done by organizers then that's the accomplishment. The other kind of call through the seven sisters is that they are obviously bridging the . . .

FW: . . . Third World gap?
TCB: Yeah, that, but also the political worldview and the artistic worldview, which has always been a tradition in our community. They are ob-

viously reaching also for Third World coalitions, which is the struggle we really haven't explored. When we talk about coalitions, it always seems to be about black and white. I think that's a real waste. So, that's another kind of call. And, three, is the Southwest Community Infirmary. Those workers are attempting to merge the best of so-called traditional medicine with the most humane of so-called modern medicine.

When you say, "What am I trying to accomplish?" I think the questions I'm raising or the gaps I'm pointing to become an assignment, so to speak, for community organizers. If that message is clear to people who work on the streets and who work with groups, then I've accomplished what I set out to do.

FW: Looking at those three calls briefly, there have been attempts and some successes at Third World coalitions. And having traveled throughout the Third World yourself, I'm sure you know that in the Third World there are a lot of people who feel an affinity for the struggles of African Americans and in the cases of people such as Robert Williams, that affinity has been an actual working together. With that in mind, do you think then that part of your call for what is needed is a validation that this is not something that is foreign to our experience? In other words, we are not asking people to do something new . . .
TCB: . . . that's so strange. Right. Because certainly there has been with the runaway captives . . .

FW: The Seminoles . . .
TCB: Yes, the Seminoles. During the sixties we had the Young Lords and the Panthers on the East Coast, and Asian student unions working with black student unions and that kind of thing, but I'm trying to get at something a little more than that. It's not only a common . . . well, it's not only a call to unite to wrath or to unite to vision, but there's also an awful lot in our own cosmology that is so similar that it's really striking. That suggests to me that if the warriors and the medicine people were merged that you would tap into a potential that is stunning.

FW: So, you're saying then that you're not calling for a union of two differ-ent groups but rather a recognition of the commonness in the two? Going to the question of the merging of the warriors and the healers, is this part of the meaning of the Korean masseur in the Academy of the Seven Arts?
TCB: He functions in a number of ways. Everything in the book, the way

it's structured, the avoidance of a linear thing in favor of a kind of jazz suite, the numerous characters, the potter and the masseur, everything becomes a kind of metaphor for the whole. We have to put it all together. It deals with all the senses and also different kinds of ways to meditate, different kinds of ways to tap into the center. The masseur, in my mind, is the other half of the potter, in the sense that to raise the clay you've got to get the clay centered. The potter's wheel is part of the whole discussion of circles, prayer circles and being in a circle. The masseur says, "My dance is my meditation." He's trying to get Obie center as Obie keeps sliding all around the table. It's just another way at trying to get at the need to get centered. It's repeated throughout the book.

When Velma is in the marshes and she thinks how did she get there, she was talking to Jamahl whose answers to the so-called problem always lie in someone else's culture. She is convinced that the trip is in the people and it's to stay centered in your own best traditions that will keep you in touch with the best of yourself.

FW: Which goes back to the point that you're not actually calling for a coalition as much as a recognition of commonness. For some people, the attempt at a coalition has resulted in a denial of self and adoption of a whole alien culture . . .
TCB: . . . of someone else's interests, someone else's agenda.

FW: Which is exactly the opposite of what you are calling for?
TCB: Right.

FW: Do you think fiction is the most effective way to do this?
TCB: I don't think fiction is the most effective way to do it. The most effective way to do it, *is to do it!*

FW: Well, what makes you think that fiction is an effective way to lay this call out there? For example, why didn't you write an essay?
TCB: Because I don't know how to write an essay, seriously. It's not that I think literature is a "deep, paramount tool for transformation," but I think it has potency and it's what I know how to do. Literature is what I do.

It took me a long time to get around to that. I never thought . . . well, writing seemed like a frivolous way to participate in struggle. It wasn't really until I went to Cuba—although I certainly had been writing for years and publishing for years, and taking some things about it rather seriously, and being embarrassed about the amount of time I used to spend trying to learn how to write—but in Cuba everything was confirmed. People made me look at what I already knew about the power of the word, which is something I certainly knew, having grown up on 125th Street and Seventh Avenue. I think it was in 1973 when I really began to realize that this was a perfectly legitimate way to participate in struggle. I don't have to be out there running in the streets or at the barricades. This counts too.

FW: So then, to talk about your career as a writer, this phase is more than just a search for a new language, it's a search for a language to be able to say something meaningful . . .

TCB: . . . to enlarge a certain kind of vision that I've been getting at in little pieces. From *Gorilla* to *Sea Birds* was a five-year span. In that five years a lot happened. I went to Cuba, I went to Vietnam. I got more deeply into community organizing. I got a certain amount of miseducation behind me and got a more serious kind of self-education. I think what is most noticeable in the widening of the lens is that in *Gorilla* those kids share with us those lessons that they learned on the block as though we the reader and writer were neighbors on the block. When I get to *Sea Birds*, I'm looking at more than that. I'm looking at all those forces that impact on us, particularly socioeconomic and political forces. But then, by the time I get to *Salt*, which is a two-year difference, I'm not satisfied with just the physical forces, I want to look at all the forces that impact.

FW: One person I know commented that there were no white people in the novel, which is not quite true . . .

TCB: . . . no, it's not . . .

FW: But that was the sense that they got. I also got a sense that this was a very expansive but still interior sort of conversation or meditation. What you were talking about was not so much what others do to us and how others do it to us, but rather what we must do for ourselves.

TCB: Yes.

FW: The colonial response: first, you have colonialism and then you have anticolonialism, which is still not affirmative of yourself because you're just reacting to your oppression and are still using colonialism as a reference.

TCB: I think that's the politics of despair and I don't ascribe to that at all. There was something before colonialism and there is something that persists in spite of it. It's that core that interests me. Colonialism was just a moment in our history. It's a very temporary thing.

FW: What you're saying then is that as long as we consider colonialism the major aspect of our reality we have in fact missed . . .
TCB: . . . we have in fact collaborated . . .

FW: . . . with colonialism because then we are implicitly saying that's where our history started . . .
TCB: . . . saying that this is our reality. It's not our reality. One of things that . . . I think it's Fred the bus driver, who is very much off-center but there have been enough people in his life to kind of spin him back, well, he's thinking about Jimmy Lyons. Jimmy Lyons would say, "colored people, Negro people are fours. The thing about fours is that if they invest too much time looking at how they are boxed in on all four sides, they never look up and know that they can build upward." To constantly be looking at those four sides is to stay in prison, is to collaborate with your captives, indeed, is to lend them energy, which is the same thing as providing them with the power to keep you locked in.

FW: In our music there has always, at certain points, been innovators who have provided the key which, once that key is presented, we can go on to another level . . .
TCB: They broke it open, yeah. That is characteristic of our everything here. You don't accept the constraints. You try to break past. Coleman Hawkins picks up the sax and rescues it from the vaudeville nonsense role that it was supposed to play. He liberates the sax from that role. He had to liberate the instrument from its own constraints in order to break something open. Jimmy Blanton picks up the bass and he opens it up for everybody. It's a whole new thing.

FW: Yeah, there're more than three octaves.
TCB: It's a whole new thing. That's true of everything. It's true of the music, it's true of our literature.

FW: The question I'm getting at is: do you think that, because of some very real constraints which were not spoken to directly enough in the late sixties and early seventies, do you think that it will be some of the women writers who will knock the hardest at trying to find some of these keys?

TCB: I don't know but I'm somewhat interested in what black women and other women, particularly young women . . . I'm interested in that particular voice and stance that they're trying to find. I think that perhaps they have a greater stake in trying to find a new vocabulary of images . . .

FW: . . . in making change.

TCB: Yeah. I think they have a really tremendous contribution to make because no one else has their vantage point. No one moves in the universe in quite that way, in all the silences that have operated in the name of I don't know what: "peace," "unity," and some other kind of bogus and ingratiating thing . . .

FW: You mean from the self-silences to the "shut-ups!"

TCB: Yeah. Yeah. Once you break that silence, then anything is possible. There's no telling where it might go. It's stunning, it's very stunning.

FW: My evidence for that and the data I'm building on is not simply what has happened in literature or the case with *The Salt Eaters*, but also if you look at film, particularly what happened with Cuban film where it was Sara Gomez (a black lower-class Cuban woman filmmaker) who really . . .

TCB: . . . broke that open. Yeah.

FW: It is the Third World woman of color, in fact the lower-class, Third World woman of color who has, after all the various liberation movements have gone on through the late sixties and seventies . . . who still remains oppressed and exploited and whose voice is still not fully heard.

TCB: Yes. They have the greatest stake in finding a new mode, a new idiom . . .

FW: . . . a new language.

TCB: Yeah.

FW: And we will all benefit from it.

TCB: Right.

FW: Thank you.

An Interview with Toni Cade Bambara

Kay Bonetti/1982

This is a print version of a recorded interview with the author, produced for sale by The American Audio Prose Library, Inc., © 1982. P.O. Box 842, Columbia, MO 65205. Reprinted with permission.

Kay Bonetti: In your preface to *Gorilla, My Love* you raise several issues in a lighthearted and comic fashion that are actually pretty serious about the relationship between the writer and his work and the writer and life around him. First of all, do you really believe that there is such a thing as "straight up fiction"?

Toni Cade Bambara: It depends on what genre you're working in. In the essay form one expects the writer to step forward and present things from the actual world so to speak. In fiction many writers make use of memory or craft, second-hand, third-hand, hearsay, overheard experiences or can deal strictly out of the head. I mean, absolutely summon up characters that have no reference in that writer's world.

I tend to leave real people alone. I'm really respectful of people's privacy. My characters of course are based on or something like people that I do know. For example, in the first collection *Gorilla, My Love* most of the children who are generally the protagonist or even the narrator in many of the stories are like particular kids that I knew—tough little compassionate kids that I love. I have tremendous respect for that kind of person but there is no kid in particular. The events that are made use of in the stories, setting, places like that, are places that I've been to or maybe heard about or sometimes the landscape is just completely out of the head or may come from dream life.

Whenever the question is raised at readings or in workshops, it always strikes me as off center. The question isn't to what degree is the work autobiographical but what do you do with, how do you transform actual experiences you've been through? How do you transform people you have encountered in order to make useable whatever lesson it is that you have abstracted from that experience that you want to lift up and share with other people? That then becomes a craft question. Although for me it's still a moral question too. A question of etiquette.

Kay Bonetti: Is there such a trend now for the true life novel, or para-journalism [creative non-fiction]? I take it that you do have strong feelings about the morality of such use of real people.

Toni Cade Bambara: For example, it would never occur to me to impale my mother on a pen or to capture relatives in ink, or reduce friends to still life, which is essentially what happens with writers who are a little careless. I think about how writers make use of people around them which is why so many people are wary around writers. You never know to what extent you're being used up.

But the question has really hit me a lot lately because I'm attempting to put into some kind of perspective what has been happening in Atlanta, Georgia, these past two years via the children's murders. What we've gotten is the media story or the media version. We've gotten the police version but we've yet to get the domestic version or the community story. And in the new book [eventually published as the novel *Those Bones Are Not My Child*] I'm trying to document what took place here in Atlanta the last two years but in a fictional stance. A lot of problems arise in the writing because of the contradictory pull of the documentary impulse and the fictional impulse. But the reason I'm creating fictional characters is so I can get at the story. The fictional characters allow me to pursue the various theories about the murders. It allows me to lift up the community voice without hustling anybody; without bringing onstage actual people and putting words in their mouths or attributing motives to them that they may not have had when they made certain kind of public statements.

So the book is kind of the combination of public statement by public figures indicating what they had actually said. The fictional characters provide me with a point of entry into the community story. It's a very hairy problem.

Kay Bonetti: In your own case, is there a discernable source or a germ that you can identify? Like a "voice" that comes to you?

Toni Cade Bambara: Different stories have different sources. Poets for example frequently hear a line, just a hip line and they may play with it; chew on it all day for a week and they really just like that line. And then they'll just build a whole poem around it just to give it a setting, just to have an occasion for getting that line off.

Some stories have, for me, very clear memories in terms of source. For example, the title story from the second story collection, *The Sea Birds Are Still Alive*, came out of anecdotes and tales and stories that people in Vietnam and Laos shared with me in the summer of '75 [1975] when I was visiting Southeast Asia. There is a line for example (I think the narrator is really saying it), in a section where the little girl resists torture and resists interrogation because she remembers that the old folks had taught her that that's the wonderful thing about revolution: you can amend past crimes and be human again; what you do and don't do matters very much for the ancestors and for the current contemporary people and for the yet unborn children. And that line actually came from an old revolutionary that I interviewed somewhere [in Vietnam].

The title story of the first collection, *Gorilla, My Love*, is about betrayal; it's about the careless way in which grownups violate the contract between grownups and children. In the story the uncle promised a little girl that he would marry her when she grew up and he was just teasing and playing but she was quite serious. That story had its source in an event that occurred in New York, Brooklyn, about 1950 something. I had gone to a puppet show that the children were putting on. The children were all ready with their puppets. A lot of the children were sitting in the front row, they were all ready to begin but the adult coordinator of the program kept looking at her watch and saying, "We'll wait a few more minutes for the people to get here." And this kind of bewildered the children who thought they were people and thought that they were important enough to start their own program. And that started me thinking how often we commit that, that kind of nonchalant little murder because kids are kids and they are little and they can't take us to court.

Kay Bonetti: In what sense could Minnie Ransom in *The Salt Eaters* be seen as an artist figure, or a creative figure?

Toni Cade Bambara: Well Minnie Ransom of course was a healer. And I see no particular difference, at least in my mind and in my work, between the medical arts, the martial arts, and what they call the lively arts. I don't know anything livelier than the martial arts quite frankly (That is to say in terms of life and death).

She is a healer and to that extent she's like a poet because poets are community health workers. I mean, it is their job to call people to something higher than a fish sandwich and a job. And certainly poets in my own cultural traditions have been regarded as priests and therapists and healers. I think to that extent that Minnie Ransom might be regarded as an artist or an artist figure. But she is what she is—she's a healer. She's just this crazy old swamp hag down there in Georgia trying to find out from her patients if they're really serious about being whole, about being healthy because it's quite a responsibility.

Kay Bonetti: But she's also an orderer of chaos in a spiritual and mental sense, is she not? And different from the more direct, upfront voice of *Gorilla, My Love*? The fictional universe in *The Salt Eaters* is one of sound, of some sort of spiritual/intellectual/psychological form that manifests itself in various ways, in auras, in essences, and also in voices. And part of what Ransom is able to do as a healer is pull in and focus on the subject at hand, so to speak.

Toni Cade Bambara: All the characters in *Salt Eaters* are part of that metaphor. The masseuse, the person doing the pottery, the martial arts people, the political theorists, the medicine people are all part of that ordering impulse. I mean lots of other people are compelled to create order, to override that seeming chaotic contradictory contrary stuff that we have to negotiate with every day. I think it's no less for an artist than it is for a political theorist, medical arts person, a mama, or anybody else.

Kay Bonetti: I guess I was thinking too in terms of the kind of writer you describe yourself as being, the way you use the phrase "straight up fiction," suggesting that school of artists who see themselves somewhat as mediums.

Toni Cade Bambara: I think that accounts for what you put your finger on a little while ago, which is the shift in voice or the very different kind of voice that we hear or are aware of in *The Salt Eaters* the novel as opposed to some of the short stories in *Gorilla, My Love*. I'm trying to get at—I was trying to get at but didn't quite pull it off—a new kind of narrator in fiction. We've had the narrator as witness, the narrator as observer, the narrator as participant; I'm after the narrator as medium, the narrator who does not claim omniscience in that arrogant way—arrogant and immoral way that is characteristic of American, particularly Euro-American that is. But I am after the narrator as a medium; a person or a force that is simply there as a kind of magnet and through that narrator people tell their stories and lay them out.

I think that comes closer to—that kind of narrator stance or narrative stance comes closer to the position the griot has in both the international African community as well as other third world communities. It's not that you step back or you oversee or you get in the middle of but you're just simply there. It's through your presence that other people can deliver up their stories and their lessons. It's rough. I'm still working at it.

Kay Bonetti: Do you have an ideal audience of the first choice when you're writing?

Toni Cade Bambara: My first audience is really the people. The characters are summoned up in order to get whatever it is told. Once in a while if you can get a nod from one of those characters, a little wink, then everything is fine. You go write on because the first relationship that has to be dealt with is the relationship between you and the work. And once that's straight and honest then the rest of it is really gravy.

The audience that gives me the most feedback tends to be folks I run across in the wash house or on a bus or on the train or just sort of traveling around. People who write little letters usually on the back of something and I think that their response is—it's straight. It's not a presentational kind of— it's not a review, it's not a critique, it's not professional; it's just a straight up gut response. I've had people stop me in the street and say, "Look, I just read something and I want to pick a bone with you about that because I don't think that happens and not only that but you left out this and what about so and so." Or people will stop me and sort of grab me by the shoulders and kiss me on the cheek and say, "I really like the way you—you really did justice to that farmer or that beauty parlor lady because nobody writes about those people and I'm glad you did that," blah, blah, blah. That kind of feedback, that kind of audience I think is my best audience.

So the problem then that faces me, faces any artist: how do you do a little Br'er Rabbit thing in terms of getting to that audience with this whole intricate, elaborate mechanism of printing and publishing and promo and critiques and reviews that gets between you and the audience that validates you, that credits you? And for me that's the community that names me, which is not to say that reviews and professional critiques aren't important and aren't usable. But it's finally the community that calls you sister or calls you daughter or calls you mama. They can either make or break you because it's only that group—I mean that's the group I'm serving. So if that audience is not reached and does not find anything usable there's almost no point in doing it.

Kay Bonetti: In the past few years, I have become aware of "third world" concerns, "third world" literature, and the function of the artist in that world. To what extent do you see being black in America as being part of the entire third world?

Toni Cade Bambara: I identify internationally. That is to say the rest of my family on the continent of Africa is here (particularly in the South), in the Caribbean, in Brazil (particularly in Bahia). The African family is worldwide. And to that extent I tend to have an international perspective because I'm concerned about everything that happens to the family.

In terms of other communities of color, both nationally and internationally, particularly as it gives rise to a group like the Seven Sisters in the novel *Salt Eaters*, one of the calls that I'm trying to make in that book among other things is coalition. I do identify with black America very, very strongly. That's my base. But the home base is still the continent, the world.

I'm concerned particularly with any member, group, or family within the world of color that is attempting to—attempting to earn its right to create history again by having control (economic, political, social, spiritual, aesthetic control) of their own country again.

Kay Bonetti: What do you view as the function of the artist?

Toni Cade Bambara: The task of the artist is determined always by the status and process and agenda of the community that it already serves. If you're an artist who identifies with, who springs from, who is serviced by or drafted by a bourgeois capitalist class then that's the kind of writing you do. Then your job is to maintain status quo, to celebrate exploitation or to guise it in some lovely, romantic way. That's your job. If you are a writer in Cuba, postrevolutionary Cuba, your job is to celebrate the triumph of the national will. If you're a writer coming out of Kenya, the postindependent era in Kenya, your job is really to critique the failure of class struggle in Kenya and to tell the truth and to try and share a vision of what that society should be like if they're gonna really liberate themselves.

As a cultural worker who belongs to an oppressed people my job is to make revolution irresistible. One of the ways I attempt to do that is by celebrating those victories within the black community. And I think the mere fact that we're still breathing is a cause for celebration. Also my job is to critique the reactionary behavior within the community and to keep certain kinds of calls out there: the children, our responsibility of children, our responsibility to maintain some kind of continuity from the past. But I think for any artist your job is determined by the community you're identifying with.

But in this country we're not encouraged and equipped at any particular time to view things that way. And so the artwork or the art practice that sells a capitalist ideology is considered art and anything that deviates from that is considered political propagandist, polemical or didactic, strange, weird, subversive, or ugly.

Kay Bonetti: Would you be comfortable being called something of a utopian writer, or being seen in that tradition?

Toni Cade Bambara: Absolutely not. No, I don't identify with the utopian literature tradition. There are several features of that kind of literature. One, it takes a satiric stance about the current society. I'm not so much satiric; I'm critical but not satiric. For satire you need a certain kind of sneering temperament and that's a little far removed from me. Another feature of the utopian literature is that it presents a vision based on the assumption that the reader and writer share a common set of values. I do not identify with most utopian literature—it does not speak to the world as I know it. It does not speak to the international scheme of things.

Another feature of utopian literature is that it doesn't look at process. It also doesn't attempt to look at this new society as part of a historical continuum. I find that a little stupid. And finally its most characteristic feature is that it is very futuristic looking. I'm also future oriented but it has to do with memory. It has to do with what I know is possible because it already happened or people need not be corrupted and perverted because I know in the past that people were not. My glance is both a back glance as well as a flash forward.

No, I wouldn't identify myself as a utopian writer. When I look at my work at any little distance the two characteristics that jump out at me is this tremendous capacity for laughter but also a tremendous capacity for rage. And the rage is usually about the almost gratuitous injustice that people have to deal with. I think, particularly of what happened here in this country in the fifties, as part of that Cold War ideology in which there was a relentless drive towards cultural conformity. If all communities in this country (and there are at least thirty-two distinguished and distinct cultures in this country) could all just forget everything, just sort of embrace collective amnesia and instead embrace this mediocre, bleached out, kinesthetically impoverished thing called popular culture that was being systematically fashioned so that big business could get at us better through entertainment and spectacle. I just despair when I consider how quickly people gave up the best of themselves so that by the time you hit the early sixties there was no particularity anymore. I'm exaggerating tremendously but there was a tremendous co-option of vibrant cultures by the commodities structure in this country.

You asked me earlier about sources with stories. That story "Broken Field Running" came about because I was doing an essay on environmental design and urban design, particularly architecture and noticing the way in which kitchens got legislated out of existence. This meant if kitchens were the headquarters of the elders and if you no longer had kitchens you didn't have your elders in your house anymore. Also, benches were removed from in front of low-income projects. If you don't have benches you don't have places for mom and pop Johnson to sit down or the old guys to play cards or dominoes and drink beer and keep surveillance of the turf and develop some sense of community sovereignty because they're out there.

The first group to go are the elders; you put them in old age homes and forgot about them, then you cut off your critical tie with the past.

Kay Bonetti: To me the most central thing that I see in your work is the whole subject of children. Children as characters, children as narrators, children as protagonists—which is actually rather unusual in western literature.

Toni Cade Bambara: I don't know what to make of that. I mean I don't have anything usable to say about the presence of children in my work. As a matter of fact, a lot of people called after reading *The Salt Eaters* once or twice to say they observed there aren't many children running around in that story and why is that? I hadn't been aware of that because I'm not aware of the children being so central in other stories except in that first collection. It is rather unusual. I've noticed that most writers—I'm thinking about writers like Walter Dean Meyers that focus on juveniles—tend to be put in the juvenile market and adult readers somehow don't realize that's fine literature. They just sort of shuttle him off somewhere in the corner. Or other people that write about children either get stuck in the juvenile market or children's books—regardless if the book might be an adult book—it's always compared to Huck Finn or Holden Caulfield. So there were no other traditions of children as protagonists, as heroes.

Kay Bonetti: Your protagonist in "Broken Field Running" says, "We blind our children. Blind them to the potential, the human potential, cripple them, dispirit them. Cripples make good clients, wards, beggars, victims." And what you say about the schools just brings me to my knees.

Toni Cade Bambara: We tend to appeal to the worst in children I think. I see four kinds of models in education. One that starts with a premise that children are public enemy number one; that they're an absolute menace to life and limb and they must be diffused and made obedient and novatized. So we get the schools that appeal to shame, to guilt where the motto seems to be you oughtta be ashamed. The children come out obedient, true believers and can be delivered up to the first demigod that comes along because they're not encouraged and equipped to think critically or to voice opinions or raise questions.

Then you have a kind of school that starts with a premise that children are innocent, that is to say stupid, and immoral and illiterates and they must be protected from certain kinds of information. And so you lie to them. Parents might say don't be afraid to go the dentist; the dentist won't hurt you. Isn't it better telling the kid what is likely to happen at a dentist so the kid can mobilize his or her own resources for the situation? But in those schools that start with protect the kid, don't let them know anything, you get more illiterates. You get more kids who don't know how to process information, who don't know how to think critically; who can't think better than they were taught and they will wind up kind of bumbling around being innocent.

Next you get a kind of school that started, I guess, in the sixties called progressive schools, so-called alternative schools that start with a good premise. They start with the premise that this society does not free up children but oppresses them. So far so good. They are about freeing up the children, not stifling the creative expression. So far so good, but most of those schools never had any sense of social theory, of, well, what do you train children for? Do you have any vision of what a good society is? So in most of those so-called alternative schools, you get kids running around on top of the tables, throwing food all over the floor, and you get teachers who are permissive mainly because they are scared. They will not take responsibility for setting standards, you know. And then you go to the meetings and the group leader is laying out earth-shaking questions like: "If the child is sitting there masturbating in front of the class in the front row, um, how do you handle this?"

And they go into this long intricate, convoluted, you know, *whatever* about the kid who's picking his nose, or whatever this kid is doing. Then one—maybe one teacher can break through and say, "I would say, hey, sweetheart, stop picking your nose. Stop playing with yourself. And then we'd get on with the lesson."

But finally there's a fourth model in this country that I'm sure exists, I hope it exists, in other communities but certainly at the Pan-African pre-schools in the black community. It starts with the premise that children are responsible, competent, efficient, and principled. In which case, in those schools, kids are encouraged to raise questions. They're encouraged to take on responsibility. They're encouraged to critique everything they read, everything they see, and they don't just sit passively and watch television. They try to dialogue with the sensibility behind a commercial, with the sensibility behind *Goldilocks and the Three Bears*, or with the sensibility behind a movie. But for the most part—that kind of school is few and far between. For the most part, we just cripple the kids.

Kay Bonetti: I'm also very interested in your metaphor of the salt eater itself. The salt eater appears, again, in that story, "Broken Field Running." In there, it's a metaphor of history gone wrong, and it's sort of implicitly given a different treatment in the novel *The Salt Eaters.* Can you explain the metaphor of the salt eater as you see it?

Toni Cade Bambara: Yeah, in the novel it's more of a dialectic. There were times when we're given the positive savior, the savior of salt. And other times the debilitating character of salt. But it finally all goes back to the African flying myth that used to be very much present in some of the old anthems in Baptist songs, particularly in songs about Ezekiel seeing the wheel. And some writers have attempted to make use of that myth, Toni Morrison, certainly, in *Song of Solomon.* And Gayl Jones in a one-act play she did called "The Ancestor."

But as the old folks tell it, we got grounded because we ate too much salt. But as *some* of the old folks say, we got grounded because we opened ourselves up to horror, to certain kinds of horror, we invited it onto the Continent and then that created tears, occasion for tears, and it was *that* salt that finally drowned our wings and made us earth-bound.

In the novel, *The Salt Eaters*, there's a section in which we look at the infirmary, the Southwest Community Infirmary, and at the old tree. And I had taken a line, I had removed the line from the manuscript before it went to press because I assumed that it was part of everyone's knowledge, but I had to put it back in because people let me know that I was out of my mind.

Let me just read that section: "They passed the infirmary where the woods began and there was old tree, where Minnie Ransom, the healer, daily placed pots of food and jugs of water for the loa, the laws alive, the spirits, that resided there. Old tree, the freed coloreds of Claybourne, had planted in the spring of 1871, the elders in coarse white robes gathering around the hole with digging sticks, the sun in their eyes. They planted the young sapling as a gift to the generations to come and as a marker in case the infirmary could not be defended and would not hold.

"Old tree, its roots fed by the mulch and compost and hope, the children gathered from the district's farms, nurtured further by the lower, called up in exacting ceremonies, under the gaze of the elders until they buzzed and a bought permanent residence, waiting. The sapling shooting up past the iron and wire and string armature, those first few springs 'til the roots took hold and anchored and the spinal column straightened to tower upward from earth to sky, from soil to rain clouds, even when the building had been raided and burnt to the ground and salted over as Rome did Carthage so long ago when they finally conquered Hannibal. Salted it over, but still we rise. Old tree."

The other thing that the elders say about eating salt (and they were making reference to Hannibal and his elephant), was that even though that whole society was supposedly wiped out and razed to the ground, and the earth salted over so nothing else could grow, that community, those people, did rise again. So we always have this image of people eating through the salt in order to fly again.

So I'm kind of turning the thing completely around on its head. By the time you get to the end of the book, the salt, the various salt myths and the various aspects of the African flying myth that have to do with salt have made a complete revolution.

Kay Bonetti: To what extent, in fact, is literature in print now reaching the audience that you would wish it to be reaching?
Toni Cade Bambara: It's difficult, which is why, within the small press community in particular, I'm thinking of [chap] books and, two-dollar paperbacks in particular, many of us have had to do very creative things in terms of reaching that audience. Book fairs, readings, not only readings on campuses, but readings in barbershops, bookstores, on the corner, in churches, in basements, library auditoriums, and pool halls.

That's certainly one way. I'm not all that committed to print, however. I think it's just one small vehicle that has some potential. I'm more inclined to think that that in a particular audience (that I consider my prime audience) that the best way to reach them would be through film. And I don't mean Hollywood film, but through independent films, which certainly are being produced in this country and throughout the world, particularly in the third world—so-called third world.

But the problem there is a distribution network. How do you bypass Hollywood distributors that firewall your films, or create a network amongst churches, library auditoriums, barbershops, and beauty parlors, and reach the people that you're really working for?

It just means there's a lot of work besides the writing. A lot of writers, particularly I'm thinking about workshops I've been conducting lately, think that once you've gotten the manuscript polished and edited that you're through. They think you send it out, you know, and it gets published, and you're through. No, it's not through, that's just step one. That's the easiest part, probably. The hardest part, that requires the work and imagination and energy and stamina and endurance is doing that little Br'er Rabbit number, and getting past book sellers who don't want your books, and getting past publishing companies who bury your book (or shred it), or getting past that whole promotional salesman network to actually reach your audience. It just requires a lot of footwork. But I think it's possible. One can do it. It just takes a lot of energy. But I don't think books are in competition with TV, or in competition with films. I think it's just another way to experience certain things.

Kay Bonetti: What has been your history in terms of publishing? You mentioned that you're out of the small press tradition?
Toni Cade Bambara: Now that I think about it, I have published very little in the small press journal. For reasons I don't quite—I can't fathom at the moment. I guess *perhaps* it's because I've been very lucky in terms of major publishing ventures. I've gotten a lot of stories in school readers, put out by major publishing houses, and the books have been taken very quickly. I've gotten contracts on those very quickly without too much sweat and jumping up and down and foaming at the mouth.

It's only now and then that I might send a story out to a small press, and I think it has to do with timing, because they will tie up your work, you know, for years and years, because there's such a backlog of stuff they have to read, and those small press journals are out of pocket, one-woman or one-man shows. So it's very difficult for them to get at the work.

I began publishing in the 1950s, when I was still in college, at a time when

I was not taking writing particularly seriously; maybe because it was so joyous a thing. I didn't think of it as serious work. I mean, if I'm not scrubbing socks on a laundry board, with bleeding knuckles, I don't think it is work.

In 1964, though—I usually read this in reviews, so I guess they must be right, because they do their homework better than I do—I got a story in *Negro Digest*, and that same month there was a story in *Massachusetts Review*. And since that time, the publishing has been fairly steady.

I was the book reviewer, the regular book reviewer, for *Liberator Magazine* from '66 to its demise in 1972. And the first collection, *Gorilla*, those stories, that book came out in 1972, but those stories date from 1955 to 1972, and the majority of them had been published before.

I don't have any big quarrel about publishing. It's only been in the last few years that I've gotten very serious about writing, that is to say writing has gotten very serious with me. Writing has become, more and more, a central activity in my life. Previously I'd always thought of myself as a teacher who writes, a social worker who writes, a youth worker who writes, a mother who writes. Now I'm a writer. I think in the next few years I may experience some difficulty in publishing simply because the output is so much more, in terms of volume, than in the past years, but I've just been lucky.

I grew up in New York. I grew up with people who were interested in books. They eventually went into publishing and became copy editors, or editors, or journalists, or something. And since I was right there—I couldn't miss. Now that I'm in Atlanta, however, [laughter] I think it might get a little hairy as time goes on.

Kay Bonetti: What role does an editor play for a writer once you are more or less established, or at least you have published one or two books? You've mentioned for instance that Toni Morrison is your editor at Random House. Are there demands put on you now that you've written *The Salt Eaters* to have another novel ready to go within a certain length of time, or anything like that?

Toni Cade Bambara: No, for the writer and the editor there are at least fifty different kinds of relationships you can establish. The one that I tend to establish, being who I am, is leave me alone. I write at my own pace. I write only what I want to do, or what I'm compelled to do. And, you know, I just sort of take it easy.

Once in a while—there was a lot of discussion about why I was a short story writer, exclusively, when the whole market is geared up for a novel. All the critics are geared up for a novel, the reviewers are geared up for the novel, teachers are geared up for the novel. It's sort of a kind of suicide, professional suicide.

But since I don't think of writing as a career, it's simply one of the ways I do my work in the world. I never paid it too much attention until I discovered that the short story I was writing was getting longer and longer, and it looked like it was going to be a novel. And I got a lot of support from Toni Morrison, my editor, about doing it.

But the relationship that we have, which I think is ideal for *me*, but probably would not work with other editors, or with other writers, is that she generally leaves me alone. Every once in a while she'll call and say how are you? We talk to each other because we're friends, and because we're very much interested in each other's work, as women, and as members of the same community.

Once in a while she may probe to find out what I'm doing, and I might send her something, and we talk contract for a minute, and the contract is done, and I hand in a copy. She usually reads it herself, makes some comments, she might make a few suggestions, which I take or not take.

And then she turns it over to her copy editor; she trains the best of the best in the business. Any copy editor that has worked under her knows what they're doing; when they leave her they can become an editor immediately. The copy editors go over it, and they catch things like I may have changed someone's age, or if this is the date then you have the wrong movie playing at the movie house, or you've changed the spelling. They might catch things like that. But for the most part, it's a very noninterference kind of activity on her part, for which I'm very grateful.

Kay Bonetti: Just now you said writing is just one of those things that is a part of your work in this world. And we've talked about the difficulties that books pose as a means of being that part of your work in the world. So I guess the question that would follow is, why do you write?

Toni Cade Bambara: I'm compelled to write. It's my meditation, I mean some people, you know, have mantras, other people go to therapists. Different people have different ways to maintain a certain kind of balance with sanity. I write because I must. If I didn't, I'd be walking around grumbling and probably be homicidal in a matter of, you know, two weeks.

I write because I really think I've got hold of something that if I share it I might save somebody else some time, might lift someone's spirits, or might enable someone to see more clearly to avoid the "okey-doke." But I do not write because it's a career or it's a profession or because the publishing industry exists. If there were no more presses and no more publishing houses, I would still be writing. I would be writing journals or I might write for readings, but I would certainly still be writing.

Kay Bonetti: Do you continually revise your work? In the story that you just read [aloud], "The Organizer's Wife," the words you read differed from my text.

Toni Cade Bambara: Oh, no. Usually when I'm through, I'm through. I'm always much more interested in whatever I'm working on at the moment. But I'm very aware that what is available to the eye isn't always available to the ear. The listening experience and the listening discipline is *extremely* different from the reading experience and the reading discipline. For example, when you're reading, the pronoun "him" may not throw you, because you know that five lines earlier you read the name, but in listening you need to hear that name, so I'll put it in.

Also, the rhythm of the eye is not the same as the rhythm of the ear, so I tend to revise a lot when I'm reading. I have reading versions of stories and written versions of stories. Sometimes it's also editing that, I mean suddenly I'm reading and I realize, oh, that doesn't make any sense. So I'd better straighten that up, clean it up, or I think of a better way to say it. But generally, once the work is done, I'm through. I write for the ear. My works are certainly very rhythmic and musical because I come out of a musical tradition.

But I'm aware that it's print. I'm very much aware of that when I'm writing. I'm very much aware of that when I'm editing. When I'm reading I try to make the work a little more performable. Although some works are certainly read with performance in mind. For example, in *The Sea Birds Are Still Alive* collection there's a story called "Medley," and it's very much written like a medley. And it's written with particular actresses in mind who like to perform my work.

Now Ruby Dee, when she first got hold of the book, *immediately* assumed that two stories in there were hers. "Witch Bird," because it's about an actress/singer, and an older woman, so she loved that. And "Medley" appealed to her because of the rhythms and the quality of person. It was the person, I think, that grabbed her. But I was very aware of writing it as a performable piece and it works better hearing than reading, than sitting down, looking at it. And as a result, Ruby took it and it became a one-woman show.

Kay Bonetti: You said a while ago that writing was simply a part of the work that you did in this world and indeed we know of several things you do. You teach, you're a mother, an activist, and have been a social worker. What part of your life does writing take, in terms of your routine? Do you set a time aside, or grab it as you can get it?

Toni Cade Bambara: There was a time when it was catch-as-catch-can, but the wonderful thing about writing a short story is that it's portable. You can walk around with it in your head. You can conjure up characters while the clothes are spinning, you can practice dialogue while you turn the, flip the pancakes, and even scribble little things on pieces of paper and stick them in mirrors and under the toothpaste glass or something.

I never get around to it [setting aside time]. If you find, you know, a vacation, or turns out you're at home, the kid maybe is away, then you write the story. But with a novel, a whole time management question came into being. The short stories are just a piece of work, but the writing novel is a way of life. So in recent years, I would say the last two or three years, writing has become far more central in my life. I organize other things around it. I write whenever I feel like it. I have no particular routine. Some days I just incubate ideas. That might go on for two or three days. I normally work in about ten or fifteen stories at a time. I may draft something, or just do a little scribbling.

I usually have one big project that I'm obsessive about, and am subject to disappear from all known postal zones on Planet Earth to get it done. With screen scripts I tend to just sign myself into a hotel for a few days with one of those Cadillac typewriters and just, you know, work. But that is not so good, because I like being at home and I like answering the phone, and talking to people, and cooking and fooling around. But now, since I've been unemployed for seven years, and only do consultant work or I might put a little program together and work for two or three weeks and then turn it over to somebody else, I'm now freed up for the first time in my life, to actually do some serious writing.

Kay Bonetti: Why have you chosen to live here in Atlanta? You were born and raised in New York City?

Toni Cade Bambara: My people are from Atlanta. My mama's folks are from Atlanta. My daddy's folks are from Savannah. I've always been very at home in the South. Atlanta has a fast airport; I can get out of here. I can get to New Orleans and, you know, eat my way across the District. I like Atlanta. One of the things I like about Atlanta is that old folks are very accessible here. I think at least 60 percent of the population are elders, and that suits me fine. I like that.

Kay Bonetti: What kind of people did you come from?

Toni Cade Bambara: Oh, we've always been working-class people. My mama was a domestic for most of her life, even after her two degrees. And then she went into civil service work. For the most part she always maintained her ties with younger people. She is what I would call a manager of intellectual resources. She's very good at spotting people and pulling out their potential.

Back in the days before we had guidance counselors and career counselors, my mother was the kind of person who watched you and then came up at you and said, "What is your plan? What do you think you gonna do in life?" And people would just deliver it up. And she would assist them.

My daddy was a runaway. He came from a long line of runaways. Men who left their family homestead to take to the road, either as musicians, or tinkers, or carpenters, or whatever. He came to the big city and lived in the bachelor societies that existed in those days in Harlem. Mostly railroad porters and shoeshine dudes, and musicians.

I get various kinds of things from both sides of the family. My mother used to take us to Speaker's Corner, 125th Street and Seventh Avenue, where we would listen to trade unionists discussing race affairs. My father used to take us to the Apollo, where we learned the *tremendously* high standards our community has for verbal performance as well as musical performance, and it was through both of them that I began to appreciate the power of the word.

Kay Bonetti: It's implicit (to me anyway) in everything you've said that as far as you're concerned, you see yourself as a black writer in black America, and by extension all of the world, so I take it that you're comfortable with the idea of a distinctively black literature?

Toni Cade Bambara: There is a distinct black literature with very particular kind of traditions. I was just thinking about that the other day. We were trying to find a copy of *Not Without Laughter* by Langston Hughes, and I was talking to Eleanor [Traylor], whom I mentioned earlier, and she was saying, "Do you realize this is the first boy," (I think the novel was written back in the forties), "first American boy who comes from a tradition?"

Now Huck Finn of course is *fleeing* Pap. I mean he is lighting out, you know, he is something to run from. And of course if Mark Twain had a little more courage Nigger Jim would have been more of the father figure that he obviously is, instead of a sort of Mammy figure that is part of the other tradition Twain has to deal with.

But just that one little aspect—it's a very distinct tradition, as opposed to

Euro-American literature, which is European to me. That is to say, the litera-ture in this country that confronts what is particular and peculiar about this country is black literature.

Everything that happens in Hemingway could happen in Europe. Any-thing that happens in Henry James *did* happen in Europe. Anything that Hawthorne or anybody's talking about could happen over there. And as Richard Wright said, if Poe and those guys were standing where *he* was standing, they would not have to *invent* horror, they would *know* it.

Black literature for me is the American literature. Now, since the 1960s, the other communities have found their voice, again, because there's cer-tainly a long tradition of Asian-American writing in this country. American literature has been thoroughly redefined in the last ten years. Quiet as it's kept, universities haven't, you know, recognized and acknowledged this fact, because universities tend to be committed to dead things, which is under-standable. I mean you can talk about Shakespeare if he's dead. You know, any findings that you come to are not going to be contradicted by a new Shakespeare work tomorrow. But it's a little harder to talk about contempo-rary work, and so they stick with the dead people.

But now you have American literature, American experience, American language, American law, being redefined. By writers coming out of the La-guna, Lakota, Rosebud Sioux, Hopi, Navajo, African Caribbean, African Af-rican, you know, I mean there's a lot of people in the country writing now.

Kay Bonetti: You mentioned coalition earlier, but do you see a future in which it's possible to have a coalition not just of, say people of color, but people of *all* colors and—
Toni Cade Bambara: People of color and people of all colors?

Kay Bonetti: Well, I mean *including* white? [Laughter]
Toni Cade Bambara: Oh—

Kay Bonetti: And different colors. [Laughter]
Toni Cade Bambara: I don't know. There's certainly has been a history of white/black coalitions or white/colored coalitions. Most of which have ended in betrayal. I'm looking particularly on the left. There's no need to look on the right, but there's certainly coalitions that have existed that have maintained credibility over the years since the 1930s in this country. Also there's certainly coalitions that were fashioned in the late 1960s that are still operating now.

Kay Bonetti: What about a coalition of readers? [Laughter]
Toni Cade Bambara: That'd be nice. That'd be interesting.

Kay Bonetti: Well, thank you very much for talking to us.
Toni Cade Bambara: Thank you.

Toni Cade Bambara

Claudia Tate/1983

From *Black Women Writers at Work*, edited by Claudia Tate (Continuum International Publishing Group, Inc., 1983). Reprinted by permission of the publisher.

Claudia Tate: What has happened to the revolutionary fervor of the sixties? **Toni Cade Bambara:** The energy of the seventies is very different from that of the previous decade. There a different agenda and a different mode of struggle. The demystification of American-style "democracy," the bold analytical and passionate attention to our condition, status, and process—the whole experience of that era led us to a peculiar spot in time, the seventies. Some say it's been a period of retreat, of amnesia, of withdrawal into narcissism. I'm not so sure. I'd say the seventies is characterized by a refocusing on the self, which is, after all, the main instrument for self, group, and social transformation.

I travel around the country a lot, and I am continually struck by the differences between the two decades. There's a difference between the apathy/retreat characterization of the seventies and what's actually going on, at least as I'm experiencing it on campuses, in prisons, in community groups. We didn't *seem* to be in a period of intense political activity as we defined its terms in the sixties. We were trained by the sixties to perceive activity, to assess movement and progress, in particular modes—confrontation, uncompromising rhetoric, muscle flexing, press conferences, manifestoes, visible groups, quasi-underground groups, hitting the streets, singing, marching, etc. On the other hand, the workings of the seventies, while less visible and less audible and less easy to perceive, to nail down and define, were no less passionate and no less significant. People attempted to transform themselves cell by cell, to organize block by block. Both seem to me essential prerequisites to broad-based organizing and clear-headed strategizing.

Unfortunately we still have not moved toward establishing an independent black political party. We still haven't clarified the issue of alliances or independent struggle. We still haven't identified the social and political imperatives of this moment or gotten a consensus regarding our domestic and foreign policy. And the eighties are now upon us—a period of devastating conflicts and chaos, a period that calls for organizing of the highest order and commitment of the most sticking kind, a period for which the sixties was mere rehearsal and the seventies a brief respite, a breathing space. Most of us are still trying to rescue the sixties—that stunning and highly complicated period from 1954 to 1972—from the mythmakers, still trying to ransom our warriors and theorists from those nuts who would cage 'em all up, crack their bones, and offer us some highly selective media fiction in place of the truth. The eighties . . . a lotta work ahead of us.

You look at what the mythmakers have done in extravaganzas like *Roots* and *King*, playing with people's blood and bones. But you just can't get overwhelmed by the massive ignorance that characterizes this racist, hardheaded, heedless society. It's a tremendous responsibility—responsibility and honor—to be a writer, an artist, a cultural worker . . . whatever you want to call this vocation. One's got to see what the factory worker sees, what the prisoner sees, what the welfare children see, what the scholar sees, got to see what the ruling-class mythmakers see as well, in order to tell the truth and not get trapped. Got to see more and dare more.

I read an awful lot—major-house books, small-press journals, offset manuscripts from local writers' workshops. I don't see the fiercesome fearlessness yet that I'd hoped to see in this period. A lot of talented, brilliant, sharp folks are out there writing. But ah . . . lotta work ahead of us.

CT: How does being black and female constitute a particular perspective in your work?

Bambara: As black and woman in a society systematically orchestrated to oppress each and both, we have a very particular vantage point and, therefore, have a special contribution to make to the collective intelligence, to the literatures of this historical moment. I'm clumsy and incoherent when it comes to defining that perspective in specific and concrete terms, worse at assessing the value of my own particular pitch and voice in the overall chorus. I leave that to our critics, to our teachers and students of literature. I'm a nationalist; I'm a feminist, at least that. That's clear, I'm sure, in the work. My story "Medley" could not have been written by a brother, nor could "A Tender Man" have been written by a white woman. Those two stories are very much cut on the bias, so to speak, by a seamstress on the inside of the cloth. I am about the empowerment and development of our sisters and of our community. That sense of caring and celebration is certainly reflected in the body of my work and has been consistently picked up by other writers, reviewers, critics, teachers, students. But as I said, I leave that hard task of analysis to the analysts. I do my work and I try not to blunder.

CT: How do you fit writing into your life?

Bambara: Up until recently, I had never fully appreciated the sheer anguish of that issue. I never knew what the hell people were talking about when they asked, "How do you manage to juggle the demands of motherhood, teaching, community work, writing, and the rest?" Writing had never been a central activity in my life. It was one of the things I did when I got around to it or when the compulsion seized me and sat me down. The short story, the article, the book review, after all, are short-term pieces. I would simply commandeer time, space, paper, and pen, close the door, unplug the phone, get ugly with would-be intruders, and get to work for a few days. Recently, however, working on a novel and a few movie scripts—phew! I now know what that question means and I despair. I had to renegotiate a great many relationships that fell apart around me; the novel took me out of action for nearly a year. I was unfit to work—couldn't draft a simple office memo, couldn't keep track of time, blew meetings, refused to answer the door, wasn't interested in hanging out in any way, shape, or form. My daughter hung in there, screened calls, learned to iron her own clothes, and generally kept out of my sight. My mama would look at me funny every now and then, finding that days had gone by and I hadn't gotten around to combing my hair or calling her to check in and just chat. Short stories are a piece of time. The novel is a way of life.

I began the novel *The Salt Eaters* the way a great many of my writings begin, as a journal entry. I frequently sit down and give myself an assignment—to find out what I know about this or that, to find out what I think about this or that when I am cozy with myself and not holding forth to a group or responding to someone's position. Several of us had been engaged in trying to organize various sectors of the community—students, writers, psychic adepts, etc.—and I was struck by the fact that our activists or warriors and our adepts or medicine people don't even talk to each other. Those two camps have yet to learn—not since the days of Toussaint[1] anyway, not since the days of the maroon communities,[2] I suspect—to appreciate each other's visions, each other's potential, each other's language. The novel, then, came out of a problem-solving impulse—what would it take to bridge the gap, to merge those frames of reference, to fuse those camps? I thought I was just making notes for organizing; I thought I was just exploring my feelings, insights. Next thing I knew, the thing took off and I no longer felt inclined to invest time and energy on the streets. I had to sort a few things out. For all my speed-freak Aries impulsiveness, I am a plodder; actually, my Mercury conjunct with Saturn is in Aries, too, so I like to get things sorted before I leap. I do not like to waste other people's time and energy. I will not waste mine.

I have no shrewd advice to offer developing writers about this business of snatching time and space to work. I do not have anything profound to offer mother-writers or worker-writers except to say that it will cost you something. Anything of value is going to cost you something. I'm not much of a caretaker, for example, in relationships. I am not consistent about giving vibrancy and other kinds of input to a relationship. I don't always remember the birthdays, the anniversaries. There are periods when I am the most attentive and thoughtful lover in the world, and periods, too, when I am just unavailable. I have never learned, not yet anyway, to apologize for or continually give reassurance about what I'm doing. I'm not terribly accountable or very sensitive to other people's sense of being beat back, cut out, blocked, shunted off. I will have to learn because the experience of *The Salt Eaters* tells me that I will be getting into that long-haul writing again, soon and often.

I've had occasion, as you can well imagine, to talk about just this thing with sister writers. How do the children handle your "absence"—standing at the stove flipping them buckwheats but being totally elsewhere? How does your man deal with the fact that you are just not there and it's nothing personal? Atrocity tales, honey, and sad. I've known playwrights, artists, filmmakers—brothers I'm talking about—who just do not understand, or maybe pretend not to understand, that mad fit that gets hold of me and makes me prefer working all night and morning at the typewriter to playing poker or going dancing. It's a trip. But some years ago, I promised myself a period of five years to tackle this writing business in a serious manner. It's a priority item now—to master the craft, to produce, to stick to it no matter how many committee meetings get missed.

My situation isn't nearly as chary as others I know. I'm not a wife, and my daughter couldn't care less what the house looks like so long as the hamper isn't overflowing. I'm not a husband; I do not have the responsibility of trying to live up to "provider." I'm not committed to any notion of "career." Also, I'm not addicted to anything—furniture, cars, wardrobe, etc.—so there's no sense of sacrifice or foolishness about how I spend my time in non-money-making pursuits. Furthermore, I don't feel obliged to structure my life in respectably routine ways; that is to say, I do not mind being perceived as a "weirdo" or whatever. My situation is, perhaps, not very characteristic; I don't know. But to answer the question—I just flat out announce I'm working, leave me alone and get out of my face. When I "surface" again, I try to apply the poultices and patch up the holes I've left in relationships around me. That's as much as I know how to do . . . so far.

CT: What determines your responsibility to yourself and to your audience? **Bambara:** I start with the recognition that we are at war, and that war is not simply a hot debate between the capitalist camp and the socialist camp over which economic/political/social arrangement will have hegemony in the world. It's not just the battle over turf and who has the right to utilize resources for whomsoever's benefit. The war is also being fought over the truth: what is the truth about human nature, about the human potential? My responsibility to myself, my neighbors, my family, and the human family is to try to tell the truth. That ain't easy. There are so few truth-speaking traditions in this society in which the myth of "Western civilization" has claimed the allegiance of so many. We have rarely been encouraged and equipped to appreciate the fact that the truth works, that it releases the Spirit, and that it is a joyous thing. We live in a part of the world, for example, that equates criticism with assault, that equates social responsibility with naive idealism, that defines the unrelenting pursuit of knowledge and wisdom as fanaticism.

I do not think that literature is *the* primary instrument for social transformation, but I do think it has potency. So I work to tell the truth about people's lives; I work to celebrate struggle, to applaud the tradition of struggle in our community, to bring to center stage all those characters, just ordinary folks on the block, who've been waiting in the wings, characters we thought we had to ignore because they weren't pimp-flashy or hustler-slick or because they didn't fit easily into previously acceptable modes or stock types. I want to lift up some usable truths—like the fact that the simple act of corn-rowing one's hair is radical in a society that defines beauty as blonde tresses blowing in the wind; that staying centered in the best of one's own cultural tradition is hip, is sane, is perfectly fine despite all claims to universality-through-Anglo-Saxonizing and other madnesses.

It would be dishonest, though, to end my comments there. First and foremost I write for myself. Writing has been for a long time my major tool for self-instruction and self-development. I try to stay honest through pencil and paper. I run off at the mouth a lot. I've a penchant for flamboyant performance. I exaggerate to the point of hysteria. I cannot always be trusted with my mouth open. But when I sit down with the notebooks, I am absolutely serious about what I see, sense, know. I write for the same reason I keep track of my dreams, for the same reason I meditate and practice being still—to stay in touch with me and not let too much slip by me. We're about building a nation; the inner nation needs building, too. I would be writing whether there were a publishing industry or not, whether there were presses or not, whether there were markets or not.

I began writing in a serious way—though I can't recall a time when I wasn't jotting stuff down and trying to dramatize lessons learned—when I got into teaching. It was a way to keep track of myself, to monitor myself. I'm a very seductive teacher, persuasive, infectious, overwhelming, irresistible. I worked hard in the classroom to teach students to critique me constantly, to protect themselves from my nonsense; but let's face it, the teacher-student relationship we've been trained in is very colonial in nature. It's fraught with dangers. The power given teachers over students' minds, students' spirits, students' development—my God! To rise above that, to insist of myself and of them that we refashion that relationship along progressive lines demanded a great deal of courage, imagination, energy, and will. Writing was a way to "hear" myself, check myself. Writing was/is an act of discovery. I frequently discovered that I was dangerous, a menace, virtually unfit to move the students and myself into certain waters. I would have to go into the classroom and beat them up for not taking me to the wall, for succumbing to mere charm and flash, when they should have been challenging me, "kicking my ass." I will be eternally grateful to all those students at City College and Livingston/Rutgers for the caring and courageous way they helped to develop me as a teacher, a person, a writer . . . and a mother, too. Fortunately, for all concerned, my daughter, a ninety-nine-year-old wise woman who travels under the guise of a young thumb-sucking kid, knows when to walk away from me, close her ears, turn my rantings into a joke, call me on a contradiction. But even after she is grown, and even if I never teach again, I will still use writing as a way to stay on center, for I'll still be somebody's neighbor, somebody's friend, and I'll still be a member of our community under siege or in power. I'll still need to have the discipline writing affords, demands. I do not wish to be useless or dangerous, so I'll write. And too, hell, I'm a writer. I am compelled to write.

CT: Do you see any differences in the ways black male and female writers handle theme, character, situation?

Bambara: I'm sure there are, but I'd be hard pressed to discuss it cogently and trot out examples. It's not something I think about except in the heat of reading a book when I feel an urge to "translate" a brother's depiction of some phenomena or say "amen" to a sister's. There are, I suppose, some general things I can say. Women are less likely to skirt the feeling place, to finesse with language, to camouflage emotions. But then a lot of male writers knock that argument out—James Baldwin trusts emotions as a reliable way to make an experience available; a lot of young brothers like Peter Harris, Melvin Brown, Calvin Kenley, Kambon Obayani have the courage to be "soft" and unsilent about those usual male silences. One could say that brothers generally set things out of doors, on open terrain, that is, male turf. But then Toni Morrison's *Song of Solomon*, angled from the point of view of a man, is an exception to that. I've heard it said that women tend to aim for the particular experience, men for the general or "universal." I don't know about all that. The notion of a street, though, is certainly handled in particular ways. To walk down the street as a woman is a very particular experience. I don't find that rendered in Ralph Ellison, Richard Wright, or John A. Williams the way I *feel* it in Gayl Jones, Sonia Sanchez, etc. But then Ann Petry's *The Street* draws me up short; I don't recognize *anybody* walking down *that* street. I've never been on *that* block; I've not *felt* that kind of out-of-itness. Finally, I guess, I just don't *believe* that woman.

In writing "The Tender Man," I couldn't wait to get Cliff and Aisha off the street and into the restaurant. I kept losing the point of view, kept sliding into the way the street resonates for Aisha, who is not the character over whose shoulder the camera looks. A brother writing that story, I suspect, would have handled the setting very differently. Aisha probably would have been less ambivalent, and Cliff's attitude toward his white wife and his child would have been rendered with a lot less ambiguity, too.

Of course, one of the crucial differences that strikes me immediately among poets, dramatists, novelists, storytellers is in the handling of children. I can't nail it down, but the attachment to children and to two-plus-two reality is simply stronger in women's writings; but there are exceptions. And finally, there isn't nearly as large a bulk of gynocentric writing as there is phallic-obsessive writings. I'll tell you—there was a period, back in 1967 or '68, when I thought I would run amok if I heard one more poem with the unzipped pants or the triggered gun or the cathedral spire or the space-missile thrust or the good f—. I'd love to read/hear a really good discussion of just this issue by someone who's at home with close textual reading—cups, bowls, and other motifs in women's writings. We've only just begun, I think, to fashion a woman's vocabulary to deal with the "silences" of our lives. I'd like to see Eleanor Traylor[3]—to my mind, the best reader/seer we've got—bring her mind to bear on the subject.

CT: Do you attempt to order human experience? Or, do you simply record experience?

Bambara: All writers, musicians, artists, choreographers/dancers, etc., work with the stuff of their experiences. It's the translation of it, the conversion of it, the shaping of it that makes for the drama. I've never been convinced that experience is linear, circular, or even random. It just is. I try to put it in some kind of order to extract meaning from it, to bring meaning to it.

It would never occur to me to simply record, for several reasons. First, it is boring. If I learn in math class that the whole is the sum of its parts, I'm not interested in recording that or repeating that. I'm more interested in finding out whether it is axiomatic in organizing people, or if, in fact, the collective is more than or different from the mere addition of individuals. If I learn in physics that nature abhors a vacuum, right away I want to test it as a law. If it is law, then my cleaned-out pocketbook ought to attract some money. Secondly, mere recording is not only boring, it is impolite and may be even immoral. If I wrote autobiographically, for example, I'd wind up getting into folks' business, plundering the lives of people around me, pulling the covers off of friends. I'd be an emotional gangster, a psychic thug, pimp, and vampire. I don't have my mother's permission to turn her into a still life. I wouldn't ask a friend to let me impale her/him with my pen or arrest them in print. I wouldn't even know how to ask permission; it seems so rude. Frequently, when I hear a good story, I will ask, "Hey, mind if I use that?" By the time, though, that I convert it my way, it's unrecognizable. Not only because I do not think it's cool to lock people into my head, my words, the type, but also because a usable truth can frequently be made more accessible to the reader if I ignore the actual facts, the actual setting, the actual people, and simply reset the whole thing. I think I hear myself saying that the third reason is that lessons come in sprawled-out ways, and craft is the business of offering them up in form and voice, a way of presenting an emotional/psychic landscape that does justice to the lesson as quickly and efficiently as possible.

I used to assign my students a writing/thinking exercise: remember how you used to get all hot in the face, slide down in your seat, suddenly have to tie your shoe even though you were wearing loafers back then in the fourth grade whenever Africa was mentioned or slavery was mentioned? Remember the first time the mention of Africa, of Black, made your neck long and your spine straight, made the muscles of your face go just so? Well, make a list of all the crucial, relevant things that happened to you that moved you from hot face to tall spine; then compose a short story, script, letter, essay, poem that make that experience of change available to the young brothers and sisters on your block.

Oh, the agony, the phone calls I got in the middle of the night, the mutterings for days and days, the disrupted whist games, the threats to my life and limb. It was hard. The notes, the outlines, the rough drafts, the cut-downs, the editing, the search for form, for metaphor. Ah, but what wonderfully lean and brilliant pieces they produced. And what they taught themselves and each other in that process of sifting and sorting, dumping, streamlining, tracing their own process of becoming. Fantastic. And I'm not talking about seasoned writers or well-honed analysts. I'm talking about first-year students from non-writing background at the City College of New York, at Livingston/Rutgers, folks who were not college-bound since kindergarten, folks who had been taught not to value their own process, who had not been encouraged, much less trained, to keep track of their own becoming. Ordering is the craft, the work, the wonder. It's the lifting up, the shaping, the pin-point presentation that matters. I used to listen to those folks teaching younger kids at the campus or at neighborhood centers, giving those kids compact, streamlined "from point A (hot face) to point B (proud)" lessons. Fantastic.

I'm often asked while on the road, "How autobiographical is your work?"—the assumption being that it has to be. Sometimes the question springs from the racist assumption that creative writing and art are the domain of white writers. Sometimes the question surfaces from a class base, that only the leisured and comfortable can afford the luxury of imagination. Sometimes it stems from the fact that the asker is just some dull, normal type who cannot conceive of the possibility that some people have imagination, though they themselves do not, poor things. I always like to dive into that one. It was once argued, still argued, that great art is the blah-blah of the white, wealthy classes. Uh huh. And what works have survived the nineteenth century? The landed-gentry tomes or Frederick Douglass's autobiography? The gentle-lady romances or the slave narratives? After I climb all over that question and try to do justice to those scared little creative writers asking out of sincere concern and confusion, I usually read my "Sort of Preface" from *Gorilla, My Love*, which states my case on autobiographical writing; namely, I don't do it . . . except, of course, that I do; we all do. That is, whomsoever we may conjure up or remember or imagine to get a story down, we're telling our own tale just as surely as a client on the analyst's couch, just as surely as a pilgrim on the way to Canterbury, just as surely as the preacher who selects a particular text for the sermon, then departs from it, pulling Miz Mary right out of the pew and clear out of her shouting shoes. Can I get a witness? Indeed. But again, the tales of Ernest J. Gaines, of Baldwin, of Gwen Brooks, whomever—the particulars of the overall tale is one of the tasks of the critics, and I am compelled to say once again that our critics are a fairly lackluster bunch. I'm always struck by that when I compare articles and speeches done by this one or that one to what comes tumbling easily and brilliantly out of the mouth of Eleanor Traylor. Do watch for her work. If there is anyone who can throw open the path and light the way, it's that sister.

What I strive to do in writing, and in general—to get back to the point I was making in direct response to your question—is to examine philosophical, historical, political, metaphysical truths, or rather assumptions. I try to trace them through various contexts to see if they work. They may be traps. They may inhibit growth. Take the Golden Rule, for example. I try to live that, and I certainly expect it of some particular others. But I'll be damned if I want most folks out there to do unto me what they do unto themselves. There are a whole lot of unevolved, self-destructive wretches out there walking around on the loose. It would seem that one out of every ten people has come to earth for the "pacific" purpose, as grandma would say, of giving the other nine a natural fit. So, hopefully, we will not legislate the Golden Rule into law.

The trick, I suspect, at this point in time in human history as we approach the period of absolute devastation and total renewal, is to maintain a loose grip, a flexible grasp on those assumptions we hold to be true, valid, real. They may not be. The world Einstein conjured or that the Fundamentalists conjure or your friendly neighborhood mystic or poet conjures may be a barrier to a genuine understanding of the real world. I once wrote a story about just that—a piece of it is in the novel, *The Salt Eaters*. A sister with a problem to solve is dawdling in the woods, keeping herself company with a small holding stone, fingering it like worry beads. It falls into a pool; she tries to retrieve it—clutching at water, clutching at water. Better to have pitched it in and stood back to read the ripples—the effects of her act. The universe is elegantly simple in times of lucidity, but we clutter up our lives with such senseless structures in an effort to make scientific thought work, to make logic seem logical and valuable. We blind ourselves and bind ourselves with a lot of nonsense in our scramble away from simple realities like the fact that everything is one in this place, on this planet. We and everything here are extensions of the same consciousness, and we are co-creators of that mind, will, thought.

CT: How have your creative interests evolved in terms of your writing?
Bambara: I don't know how to chart the evolution of my creative interest. Suffice to say that the lens has widened, the scope broadened, and the demands on myself have increased. How do we ensure space for our children was a concern out of which the stories in the first collection, *Gorilla, My Love*, grew. When my agent in those days, Hattie Gossett, nudged me and said I ought to put together some of the old stories for a collection, I thought, aha, I'll get the old kid stuff out and see if I can't clear some space to get into something else. Most of those stories are what I would call on-the-block, in-the-neighborhood, back-glance pieces, for the most part.

How are we faring now that the energy is shifting? How do we sustain ourselves between the sixties and the eighties? Out of that concern some of the stories in the second collection, *The Sea Birds Are Still Alive*, sprang. Stories like "Broken-Field Running" and "Am I Spoiling You," also known as "The Apprentice" in other anthologies, speak directly to that issue. They are both on-the-block and larger-world-of-struggle pieces, very contemporary, and much less back-glance.

How do we rescue the planet from the psychopaths? Do we have a future as sane, whole, governing people? Do we realize we are a people at the crossroads? *The Salt Eaters* is a thrown-open sort of book generated by those questions. It's on-the-block, but the borders of the town of Claybourne, Georgia, where the story is set, do not contain or hem in the story. It gets downright cosmic, in fact, in the attempt to sound the alarm about the ineptness and arrogance of the nuclear industry and call attention to the radical shifts in the power configurations of the globe and to the massive transformations due this planet in this last quarter of the twentieth century.

What seems to inform the works I'm up to my eyebrows in now—a script (whose not-so-hot working title is "Ladies-in-Waiting") about a group of women of color in 1979, 1968, 1942, 1933, getting ready to rescue or ransom their husbands, lovers, fathers, brothers from various hostage-keeping institutions; and a new collection of short stories about "families" of blood, of struggle, traveling troupes, etc.—are questions like: what alliances make sense in this last quarter? Where are the links of resistance to be forged, the links of vulnerability to be strengthened? Once again, I'm exploring ways to link up our warriors and our medicine people, hoping some readers will fling the book down, sneer at my ineptitude, and go on out there and show how it's supposed to be done. Too, I'm staying with a group of women from my novel, The Seven Sisters—a group of performing artists from the African American, Asian American, Chicano, "Puertoriquena," and Native American communities—also in hopes that sisters of the yam, the rice, the corn, the plantain, might find the work to be too thin a soup and get on out there and cook it right.

What is noticeable to me about my current writing is the stretch out toward the future. I'm not interested in reworking memories and playing with flashbacks. I'm trying to press the English language, particularly verb tenses and modes, to accommodate flash-forwards and potential happenings. I get more and more impatient; though, with verbal language, print conventions, literary protocol and the like; I'm much more interested in filmmaking. Quite frankly, I've always considered myself a film person. I am a fanatic movie watcher, and my favorite place to be these days is in a screening room, or better yet, in the editing room with those little Mickey Mouse gloves on. There's not too much more I want to experiment with in terms of writing. It gives me pleasure, insight, keeps me centered, sane. But, oh, to get my hands on some movie equipment.

An awful lot of my stories, particularly the first-person riffs and bebop pieces, were written, I suspect, with performance in mind. I still recall the old days, back in the fifties, looking for some damn thing to use in auditions. There's just so much you can do with Sojourners' "Ain't I a Woman" and trying to recast Medea as a New Orleans swamp hag. It does my heart good to have Ruby Dee swoop down on me—which she manages to do somehow, that Amazon of small proportions—for writing things like "Witchbird," an eminently performable story about a mature woman—as they say in the fashion ads—tired of being cast as mammy or earth mother of us all. I've started a lot of plays, mainly because I can't bear the idea of sisters like Rosalind Cash, Gloria Foster, Barbara O. Jones—the list goes on—saddled with crap or given no scripts at all. But finally, I think I will be moving into film production because I want to do it right; I want to script Marie Laveau for Barbara O. Jones and do Harper's Ferry with the correct cast of characters—Harriet Tubman, Mary Ellen or Mammy Pleasant, Frederick Douglass, the Virginia brothers and sisters waiting to be armed. Now can't you just see Verta Mae and Maya Angelou and William Marshall and Al Freeman, Jr., in a movie such as that?

My interests have evolved, but my typing hasn't gotten any better. I no longer have the patience to sit it out in the solitude of my backroom, all by my lonesome self, knocking out books. I'm much more at home with a crew swapping insights, brilliances, pooling resources, information. My main interest of the moment, then, is to make films.

CT: Let's look at this excerpt from the *New York Times* review on your *Gorilla, My Love*:

> Toni Cade Bambara's *Gorilla, My Love* is one of a few books published recently by black writers that fulfills the requirements of the Yeats quotation, "Only that which does not teach, which does not cry out, which does not condescend, which does not explain, is irresistible." I am tired of being shouted at, patronized, bullied, and antagonized by black writers. If I've bought their books, it means I intend to give them my attention; if I've spent $6.95 to "hear" what they have to say, I dislike being told I'm an insensitive, arrogant honky who won't listen. Toni Cade Bambara tells me more about being black through her quiet, proud, silly, tender, hip, acute, loving stories than any amount of literary polemicizing could hope to do. She writes about love: a love for one's family, one's friends, one's race, one's neighborhood, and it is the sort of love that comes with maturity and inner peace. —C.D.B. Bryan, *The New York Times Book Review*, October 15, 1972, p. 31.

Bambara: I recall that the comment about being antagonized by black writers struck me as funny. There were other white reviewers who went off their nut because I didn't get on their case, didn't seem to be paying them due attention. What the hell? The feedback, though, that has mattered is that which comes through letters or in reviews in periodicals like *Freedom Ways* and *First World* and that wonderful review—my God, it was so much better written and thought out than my book—Michele Russell did of *Sea Birds* in *The New American Movement*. Children still write and call about the Doubleday book, *Tales and Short Stories for Black Folks*, which convinced me that they are good readers and not the remedial compensatory-education, basket-case students their teachers swear they are. And every once in a while, some mama will put her hands on my shoulders, the way Alice Childress did some ten years ago—and the grip still resonates—and said, "Daughter, what you tried to do with *The Black Woman* was mighty fine. Try it again."

I'm very fortunate in that my readership is not anonymous and the feedback is personal. I meet readers on the bus, in the laundromat, at conferences, in the joint, damn near everywhere. I get letters, calls, reviews here and there, and even appear in an occasional CLA [College Language Association] or MLA [Modern Language Association] paper. It keeps me going. I've been told, of course, everything from A to Z—that all my political polemicizing is destroying whatever gift for storytelling and conjuring characters I have, or that my work is too soft, too much about ordinary people and that I ought to tackle "big" figures and "big" revolutionary events, or that it's a pleasure to read about my men and women, who don't seem to be all up in each other's face, or that I am not fearless enough, angry enough about sexist behavior in the community. Of course, everyone has a story that I should write for them. I appreciate all the feedback. Keeps me going. So finally, primarily, and ultimately, I'm not at all concerned about whether white reviewers are comfortable or ill at ease with my work. I've been told this is a foolish attitude on my part. But while I may not be very shrewd about my, ah, "lit-turrary car-rear," I am quite clear and serious about my work in the world. It's a very big place, the world. There are actually readers out there who do not take their cue from the *New York Times*; and, of course, there are millions right here in our community who don't read books at all. That's okay. I plod ahead. I do my work. I try to stay centered and not get poisoned, or intoxicated, as they say, with whatever success I've had.

CT: Who has influenced your writing?
Bambara: My mama. She did the *New York Times* and the *London Times* crossword puzzles. She read books. She built bookcases. She'd wanted to be a journalist. She gave me permission to wonder, to dawdle, to daydream. My most indelible memory of 1948 is my mother coming upon me in the middle of the kitchen floor with my head in the clouds and my pencil on the paper and her mopping around me. My mama had been in Harlem during the renaissance. She used to hang out at the Dark Tower, at the Renny, go to hear Countee Cullen, see Langston Hughes over near Mt. Morris Park. She thought it was wonderful that I could write things that almost made some kind of sense. She used to walk me over to Seventh Avenue and 125th Street and point out the shop where J. A. Rogers, the historian, was knocking out books. She used to walk me over to the Speaker's Corner to listen to the folks. Of course, if they were talking "religious stuff," she'd keep on going to wherever we were going; but if they were talking union or talking race, we'd hang tough on the corner.

I wasn't raised in the church. I learned the power of the word from the speakers on Speaker's Corner—trade unionists, Temple People as we called Muslims then, Father Divinists, Pan-Africanists, Abyssinians as we called

Rastas then, Communists, Ida B. Wells folks. We used to listen to "Wings Over Jordan" on the radio; and I did go to this or that Sunday school over the years, moving from borough to country to city, but the sermons I heard on Speaker's Corner as a kid hanging on my mama's arm or as a kid on my own and then as an adult had tremendous impact on me. It was those marvelously gifted, extravagantly verbal speakers that prepared me later for the likes of Charlie Cobb, Sr., Harold Thurman, Revun Doughtery, and the mighty, mighty voice of Bernice Reagon.

My daddy used to take me to the Apollo Theater, which had the best audience in the world with the possible exception of folks who gather at Henry Street for Woodie King's New Federal Theater plays. There, in the Apollo, I learned that if you are going to call yourself some kind of communicator, you'd better be good because the standards of our community are high. I used to hang out a bit with my brother and my father at the Peace Barber Shop up in Divine territory[4] just north of where we lived, and there I learned what it meant to be a good storyteller. Of course, the joints I used to hang around when I was supposed to be walking a neighbor's dog or going to the library taught me more about the oral tradition and our high standards governing the rap, than books.

The musicians of the forties and fifties, I suspect, determined my voice and pace and pitch. I grew up around boys who carried horn cases and girls who couldn't wait for their legs to grow and reach the piano pedals. I grew up in New York City, bebop heaven—and it's still music that keeps that place afloat. I learned more from Bud Powell, Dizzy, Y'Bird, Miss Sassy Vaughn about what can be communicated, can be taught through structure, tone, metronomic sense, and just sheer holy boldness than from any teacher of language arts, or from any book for that matter. For the most part, the voice of my work is bop. To be sure, pieces like "The Survivor" [*Gorilla*] and others that don't come to mind quickly because I can never think of titles, show I can switch codes and change instruments; and since moving South, I've expanded my repertoire to include a bit of the gospel idiom. Certainly, "The Organizer's Wife" [*Sea Birds*] and sections of *The Salt Eaters* are closer to gospel than to jazz. The title story of the last collection, "The Sea Birds Are Still Alive," would not have worked in bop, as it is set in Southeast Asia with a cast of characters that are Asian, European, South American, Euro-American, and a narrator who must remain as close as possible to a camera lens and stay out of the mix.

CT: Who have been your mentors?

Bambara: There have been a great many inspirational influences, and they continue to be so. I'm still in first gear. Addison Gayle, for example, a friend and colleague back in the early sixties, urged me to assemble a book on the black woman rather than run off at the mouth about it. It was Addison who got me the contract to do the second book, *Tales and Short Stories for Black Folks*. I can't remember who clubbed me over the head to start doing reviews for Dan Watts's *Liberator*, but that experience certainly impacted on what and how and why I write; and the support I get now from my editor and friend, Toni Morrison—well, I just can't say what that does for me. She'll feed me back some passage I've written and say, "Hmm, that's good, girl." That gives me a bead on where I am and keeps me going.

I suspect the greatest influence now, what determines the shape and content of my work, is the community of writers. While black critics are woefully lagging behind, it seems to me, not adequately observing trends, interpreting, arguing the value of products for both practitioner and audience, there is, nonetheless, a circle, if you will—not to be confused with clique, coterie, or even school of writing. But writers have gotten their wagons in a circle, which gives us each something to lean against, push off against. It's the presence on the scene of Gwen Brooks, Ron Milner, Alice Walker, and Lorenzo Thomas that helps me edit, for instance, that helps me catch myself when I blunder in the elements of the craft—a slip of voice or mask, a violation of spatial arrangement, a mangling of theme, a disconnectedness to traditions. I'm influenced by Ishmael Reed, Quincey Troupe, Janet Tolliver, Lucille Clifton, Ianthe Thomas, Camille Yarborough, Jayne Cortez, etc., in the sense that they represent a range and thus give me the boldness to go head-on with my bad self. The found voice of writers from other communities—Leslie Silko, Simon Ortiz, Rudy Anaya, Sean Wong, Wendy Rose, Lawson Inada, Janice Mirikitani, Charat Chandra, etc.—also influences my reach, my confidence to plumb our traditions, do more than just scan our terrain but stretch out there.

It's a dismally lonely business, writing. It has never given me a bad time in and of itself. I love the work; but to keep at it, I need to slap five every now and again with Pearl Lomax, Nikki Grimes, Victor Cruz, Toni Morrison, or Verta Mae, whether they're in slapping distance or not. It's not well enough appreciated, I think, what the presence or absence of certain spirits in the circle mean to keep one energized and awake. I'm always stunned, appalled, by reviewers and interviewers who don't realize this is not a popularity contest or a tournament. Not long ago, some crazy TV person was running off at the mouth about how wonderful it was to read my work as compared to this writer, that writer, as though I'd be overjoyed to hear my colleagues "murder-mouthed." It took me three beats to plant my hands safely in my pocket before taking off on the assumption, not to mention his head. That we keep each other's writing alive is the point I'm trying to make. The literature of this crucial time is a mixed chorus.

CT: Would you describe your writing process?

Bambara: There's no particular routine to my writing, nor have any two stories come to me the same way. I'm usually working on five or six things at a time; that is, I scribble a lot in bits and pieces and generally pin them together with a working title. The actual sit-down work is still weird to me. I babble along, heading I think in one direction, only to discover myself tugged in another, or sometimes I'm absolutely snatched into an alley. I write in longhand or what kin and friends call deranged hieroglyphics. I begin on long, yellow paper with a juicy ballpoint if it's one of those 6/8 bop pieces. For slow, steady, watch-the-voice-kid, don't-let-the-mask-slip-type pieces, I prefer short, fat-lined white paper and an ink pen. I usually work it over and beat it up and sling it around the room a lot before I get to the typing stage. I hate to type—hate, hate—so things get cut mercilessly at that stage. I stick the thing in a drawer or pin it on a board for a while, maybe read it to someone or a group, get some feedback, mull it over, and put it aside. Then, when an editor calls me to say, "Got anything?" or I find the desk cluttered, or some reader sends a letter asking, "You still breathing?" or I need some dough, I'll very studiously sit down, edit, type, and send the damn thing out before it drives me crazy.

I lose a lot of stuff; that is, there are gobs of scripts and stories that have gotten dumped in the garbage when I've moved, and I move a lot. My friend, Jan, was narrating a story I did years ago and someone asked, "Where can I find it?" Damned if I know. It was typed beautifully, too, but it was twenty-four pages long. Who can afford to print it? It'll either turn up or not. Nothing is ever lost, it seems to me. Besides, I can't keep up with half the stuff in my head. That's why I love to be in workshops. There are frequently writers who get stumped, who dry up and haven't a clue. Then, here I come talking about this idea and that scenario—so things aren't really lost.

The writing of *The Salt Eaters* was bizarre. I'll spare you the saga of the starts and fits and stuttering for the length of a year. I began with such a simple story line—to investigate possible ways to bring our technicians of the sacred and our guerillas together. A Mardi Gras society elects to reenact an old slave insurrection in a town torn by wildcat strikes, social service cutbacks, etc. All hell breaks loose. I'm sliding along the paper, writing about some old Willie Bobo on the box and, next thing I know, my characters are talking in tongues; the street signs are changing on me. The terrain shifts, and I'm in Brazil somewhere speaking Portuguese. I should mention that I've not been to Brazil yet, and I do not speak Portuguese. I didn't panic. It was no news to me that stuff comes from out there somewhere. I dashed off about thirty pages of this stuff, then hit the library to check it out. I had to put the novel aside twice; but finally, one day I'm walking out in the woods that some folks here call a front yard, and I slumped down next to my favorite tree and just said, "Okay, I'm stepping aside, y'all. I'm getting out of the way. What is the story I'm supposed to be telling? Tell me." Then I wrote *The Salt Eaters*. It was a trip to find the narrator's stance. I didn't want merely a witness or a camera eye. Omniscient author never has attracted me; he or she presumes too much. First person was out because I'm interested in a group of people. Narrator as part-time participant was rejected, too. Finally, I found a place to sit, to stand, and a way to be—the narrator as medium through whom the people unfold the stories, and the town telling as much of its story as can be told in the space of one book.

This business of narrating is a serious matter. Oftentimes I've been asked, "Where's your narrator?" or told, "Your narrator is always so unobtrusive unless the story is first person." Most of the time it seems that way because the narrator speaks the same code and genuinely cares for the people, so there's no distance. That suits my temperament. I am not comfortable conjuring up the folks and then shoving them around like pawns. I conjured them up in order to listen to them. I brought Virginia out, for example, the sister in "The Organizer's Wife," because I wanted to know what those quiet-type sisters sound like on the inside. It was always the quiet, country students that slipped my grasp in the classroom. When I get back to teaching, I want to be able to service them, better than I have, so I have to get the narrator out of the way. One way to do that is to have the narrator be a friend, be trustworthy.

The work in *The Salt Eaters* was far more difficult. The narrator had to be nimble, had to lend herself to different voices and codes in order to let the other characters through. There are only two sections in the whole book where something is being said, viewed, pondered, that is not in some particular character's terms: once, when we get the history of the Southwest Community Infirmary and the tree the elders planted as a marker in case the building was destroyed—originally, that section was narrated by the tree; in rewriting I had one of the loas sing it . . . either was a bit much, given all the other goings-on in the book; and then, in the cafe during a storm when the future of Claybourne is glimpsed—originally, the rain narrated that section, but that also got to be a bit much.

In my current work I'm far more disciplined and orderly. I've mapped out a collection of stories. Some are from the point of view of young men, some from elders; some are set in the States, others in the Caribbean. One is narrated by Pan—every time I see Nick Ashford, I want to do a movie about Pan and rescue that bro,' Pan I mean, from the bad press the early Christian church gave him—another by an angel. I've gotten more regular of late in my habits because my daughter asked me when, if ever, I'm going back to work. I discovered that I'd rather hang around the house so I must look like I'm working, you see.

CT: The name Hazel recurs in your work. Is there any particular reason for that? Also, the image of a gorilla is very curious.

Bambara: The first time I heard those sounds, "hay zil," my mother was stretching out on the couch, putting witch hazel pads on her eyes, and I thought, "Hmmm, witch hazel." I was fond of witches, still am, the groovy kind. I once had a belt made out of shellacked hazel nuts. But the combination—witch hazel—I was off and running. It's a powerful word, "hazel," a seven, and the glyph we call "zee" is ancient and powerful. The critic—I should say aesthetic theorist or something fancy to suit her style—Eleanor Traylor, calls me "Miss Hazel" and maintains that the Miss Hazel we meet in the story "My Man Bovanne" is the central consciousness in the whole Bambara canon. Ahem!

As for gorilla—the term has always been one of endearment. It comes up in "Raymond's Run," [*Gorilla, My Love*] and in "Medley" [*Sea Birds*] in different ways. In "Medley" it signals macho, but the charge is made with affection. While I was typing up "Raymond's Run" to send out years ago, I noticed I had the boy shaking the fence like a gorilla; and I thought, "Oh, my God, Cade! What the hell are you doing? How pro-racist!" I kept juggling that passage around. I felt uncomfortable with it but ran with it anyway. People get on my case about it—"What kind of thing is that to say about a young Blood?"—shades of King Kong and the nigger-as-ape and all. What kind of thing, indeed? They're right. I was wrong. I've some nerve expecting my personal idiolects to cancel out, supersede, or override the whole network of racist name-calling triggered by that term.

CT: What impact has the women's movement had on black women?

Bambara: What has changed about the women's movement is the way we perceive it, the way black women define the term, the phenomena and our participation in it. White bourgeois feminist organizations captured the arena, media attention, and the country's imagination. In the past we were trained to equate the whole phenomena with the agenda, the concerns, the analysis of just those visible and audible organizations. Black women and other women of color have come around to recognizing that the movement is much more than a few organizations. The movement is exactly what the word suggests, a motion of the mind.

Everybody has contributed to the shifts in mental attitude and behavior, certainly everybody has been affected by those shifts—men, women, children, here and abroad. We're more inclined now, women of color, to speak of black midwives and the medicine women of the various communities when we talk of healthcare rather than assume we have to set up women's health collectives on the same order as non-colored women have. In organizing, collectivizing, researching, strategizing, we're much less antsy than we were a decade ago. We are more inclined to trust our own traditions, whatever name we gave and now give those impulses, those groups, those agendas, and are less inclined to think we have to sound like, build like, non-colored groups that identify themselves as feminist or as women's rights groups, or so it seems to me. There's still much work to be done in terms of building protective leagues in our communities—organizations that speak to the physical/psychological/spiritual/economic/political/creative safety and development of our sisters. Also, bridges need to be built among sisters of the African diaspora and among sisters of color. I'm not adamantly opposed to black-white coalitions; there are some that speak to our interests, but I personally am not prepared to invest any energy in that kind of work. There are too many other alliances both within the black community and across colored communities, both at home and abroad, that strike me as far more crucial.

CT: On *For Colored Girls* and *Black Macho* . . .
Bambara: Before getting to critical responses and battles, I still am interested in knowing what on earth Wallace's editor at Dial Press thought he or she was doing? There is a wonderful book locked up in *Black Macho*—the story of a young woman who begins to view the women of her family in a new way, who comes down from Sugar Hill in time to catch the tail end of the sixties, who has experienced life in such a, oh, I dunno what kind of way, as to state as she does that black women have never listened to each other—

oh, I feel bad for her—who sees shortcomings in the black movement and attempts to find a home in the feminist movement. There's a fine book there. It got buried under the one we got. I, for one, however, am pleased with the one we got for all its inaccuracies and shortcomings. It has broken open a question too many of us would like to ignore, would like to leave festering; that is, the power perversities and degrading lunacies we get caught up in, in playing out the man-woman comic opera. The book is a challenge to take a hard look at the cost of machismo for the total community. It is also a challenge to sisters who did not fall back in the sixties, who did not think "prone" was/is our position, but who kept on keeping on—to set the record straight.

I've read reviews of *Black Macho* and Shange's *For Colored Girls*, heard each and both discussed on campuses, in prisons, in beauty parlors, in the food co-op, at conferences, on buses, you name it. I've heard one or both called "dirty feminists" and heard feminism equated with ball-busting anger, with mental derangement, with treason. I've also heard equally passionate discussions of each or both together that have led to intense inquiries into the dynamics of sexism, misogyny, and gynophobia, and the theory and practice of systematically or individually underdeveloping women based on the premise that women are inferior, are not worthy of equity and respect, are dangerous. I've been part of discussions about either or both that have led many sisters and brothers to the conclusion that it is not enough to take a stand against sexism; we must push each other to take a stand for feminism, for systematically and individually encouraging and equipping our women to develop power in all realms.

Of course, if Faint Heart can reduce Shange and Wallace—I hate lumping them together; I see so little resemblance—to a stereotype—evil ole black bitches—why then Faint Heart is exempt from having to deal with the alarm one's sounding, with the complexity one's depicting, with the challenge, the demand to change. Faint Heart attempts to stereotype for the same reason any other faint hearts stereotype—it relieves one from the burden of thinking, of wrestling with the vibrancy of real, live women, real live observers, who have put their fingers on real, live problems. The anger, dismay, disappointment, or just sheer bewilderment that many women experience as a way of life in regard to the man-woman setup is something we're all going to have to get used to airing. Women are not going to shut up. We care too much, I think, about the development of ourselves and our brothers, fathers, lovers, sons, to negotiate a bogus peace.

I was asked to contribute a piece to *The Black Scholar*, to respond to an article Robert Staples wrote in response to so-called angry black feminist writers. I declined. It didn't feel right. After I read the Staples piece, I wept for the brother, ya know? I mean, damn, where's he been? I read the other pieces. Sarah Fabio, as usual, knocked me out. Finally, I thought to myself, why go to sisters to comment every time some brother wants to speak his part on the issue? Let Kalamu ya Salaam answer Staples. Turn an issue of *Black Scholar* over to Peter Harris or Haki or some of the other brothers around the country trying to put a brotherhood/manhood conference together. Brothers ought to take responsibility for enlightening brothers. At this point in time I'm not even sure there's a damn thing sisters can tell brothers, ya know what I mean?

It's getting a little crazy. Brothers snarling at *Sula* 'cause Sula takes all the male prerogatives, the bold-ass bitch. If a sister had written *Jane Pittman*, there would have been a furor about that passage where the sister stands there, after what's-her-name got raped, sputtering at the men: "Dammit, would you men for once . . . can't you just . . . don't just stand there like asinine fools . . . for crying out loud . . . can't men do a goddam thing . . . go get the lantern." If a sister had written half the works of Ousmane Sembene, there'd be back-and-forth debates raging about reverse sexism: how come the heroics are always done by the women? How come the women in *God's Bits of Wood* outdo the men in courage? I'm telling you, any woman who even stumbles backwards into sexual politics is going to draw fire, at this moment in time anyway.

Whatever the case, I am happy for Ntozake. She has spirit and flair and lyricism, and I wish her well. I hope she has good people around her who will keep her on her course, and I hope we don't drive her into a ditch or over the edge. *Black Macho* is the only work I know by Wallace. I think it has accomplished good things for us. I wish her well, and I hope she'll be a lot more wary and shrewd when next she comes out with a book and realize that certain folks will attempt to throw her to the wolves.

I suspect I am getting old. A friend read my review of *Black Macho* in the *Washington Post* and jumped all in my chest: "You would've crucified her five years ago. You would have torn that book to shreds ten years ago. You would have blah, blah . . ." I dunno. A couple of writers who recently joined the Pamajo Writers Workshop were saying how refreshing it was to come to our gathering where we are not tied up in knots every second arguing the ideological correctness of this or that comma. I knew what they meant. People have to have *permission* to write, and they have to be given space to breath and stumble. They have to be given time to develop and to reveal what they can do. I'm still waiting for another Gayl Jones novel or two so I

can gauge whether I've been reading the first two correctly. There's a dyna-
mite sister in the Pamajo Workshop, Joyce Winters, and I can't wait to read
what she's going to be doing five, ten years from now. I'm not for knocking
folks out of the circle just because they make some of us uncomfortable.
There are no soloists after all; this is group improvisation. The literature
of this moment is made up of a whole lot of voices. I'm very glad Shange's
around, and I'll be glad when the smoke clears and we can step into *Black
Macho* and excavate those shards that can help us reconstruct—do some
serious changes in mind sets and actions. The truth of it is, a whole lot of
organizations back then in the sixties floundered, fell apart, and wasted a lot
of resources in the process, due in large measure to male ego, male whim,
and macho theatre. That story needs to be told. Had Wallace been a part of
the black movement, I do not doubt that she would have had the fearlessness and the data to do it. It needs getting said. We can't keep wasting each
other. There's a war going on.

CT: What advice can you share with new writers?
Bambara: Well, there's lots of advice I need to give myself and have been
trying to get from others, so I'll lay it all out.

Writers ought to form workshops, collectives, unions, guilds, for several
reasons. One, it is not fun to be so frequently alone. Two, there are a helluva
lot of things writers need to know about markets, copyright laws, marketing, managing money, taxes, the craft itself, etc., that can more easily be
mastered if people pool their resources. Three, writers get screwed right
and left in the marketplace because we are individually represented, but collectives can have as much clout with city, state, and federal arts councils as
dance companies and symphonies.

If you live in the Southeast you ought to join SCAAW, the Southern Collective of African American Writers, a regional service organization that
conducts an annual conference, publishes a monthly newsletter, holds
regular readings in the Atlanta area, hosts receptions for visiting writers,
and conducts workshops to maximize the effectiveness of writers, editors,
publishers, typesetters, and anyone else connected with books and journals.
The yearly dues is five dollars. Send same to SCAAW, The Neighborhood
Art Center, 252 Georgia Avenue, S.W., Atlanta, Georgia 30313. If you live
in a region without a collective, organize one and then contact Haki[5] at the
Institute of Positive Education in Chicago [7524, So. Cottage Grove Ave.,
Chicago, Illinois 60619], and let's all see about forming a national organiza-
tion, finally.

Get businesslike about the business of writing. Not only can you get ripped off, you can get lost. Just as musicians need to take a few law courses—not to mention karate and target practice, given the filthy nature of the recording industry—so, too, writers need to deglamorize publishing and study marketing, distributing, printing—the entire process including bookbinding.

Read a lot and hit the streets. A writer who doesn't keep up with what's out there ain't gonna be out there.

Basically, that's the advice I recite to myself at least once a month. I forced myself to organize a workshop although I hate routine in my life, and I stick closely with the development of SCAAW although it means I can't always take a gig out of the city, because I know that I will try to get it together for younger writers even if I don't for myself.

1. Toussaint L'Ouverture (1742?–1803) was the black liberator or Haiti.

2. Communities of escaped slaves in the Americas.

3. A teacher of literature.

4. An area of Harlem around Father Divine's church.

5. Haki Madhubuti (or Don Lee).

Not About to Play It Safe: An Interview with Toni Cade Bambara

Justine Tally/1985

From *Revista Canaria de Estudios Ingleses* 11 (November 1985). Reprinted by permission of Justine Tally.

Justine Tally: Barbara Christian has defined Alice Walker as a Southern writer and Toni Morrison as a Northern one, but you yourself glide in and out. You make some absolutely incredible changes of perspective from the urban to the rural areas, from the North to the South. To what do you owe this tremendous versatility?

Toni Cade Bambara: I think it's fairly common. Where one is, what kind of voices one hears, or what kind of modes one moves in, Gospel mode, Jazz mode, Blues mode, they all develop your ear. It's not peculiar to me. In looking at other writers, for example Ishmael Reed, if you look at the body of his work it's very clear when he left Chattanooga, when he left Buffalo, when he was in lower East Side New York, the California novels. I guess it has a lot to do with ear. I certainly have a trained ear, having grown up around people who are Southern, West Indian, Continental African, and certainly grew up around Blues men, Blues people, Jazz people, Gospel folk, so the different voices are familiar to me.

JT: Can you notice a change in your own writing when you move from "the sleepy South to the Be-bop North," as you have put it? Do you notice a change in your attitude while you are writing?

TCB: I noticed definite change when I moved from New York to Atlanta, a change in pace. For example, in putting the novel *The Salt Eaters*[1] together, I was depending on a story I wrote some time ago that was published in the collection *The Sea Birds Are Still Alive*[2] called "The Organizer's Wife," and it was the first time I had attempted that voice and that pace—slow, rural, the narrator as well as the characters. And I guess that story was a kind of rehearsal for *The Salt Eaters* which combines any number of kinds of voices; it's still basically "be-bop," but it gives the illusion of moving into a gospel mode.

JT: You are aware, then, of writing in a particular mode, as you say. For example, Eleanor Traylor has written an interpretation of *The Salt Eaters* as a jazz suite.[3] Do you do this on purpose? Were you aware of writing a jazz suite when you were writing *The Salt Eaters*?

TCB: When Eleanor Traylor uses the term *jazz suite*, one part of that is device. It is an attempt on her part to make the discussion manageable. So one part is device on the part of the critic. The other part is accurate description in the sense that there is enough about the structure and about the tone and about the relationship or ensemble playing of characters to justify the term *jazz suite*. But finally that's an invention on the part of the critic who wishes to collaborate with the author. I think it's very creative and it's very respectful. I think she's one of the finest critics around. I've enjoyed the work she's done on James Baldwin, on Margaret Walker, and she did a fabulous piece called "The Fabulous World of Toni Morrison" in which she collaborates with Toni's eye and her sense of fable. And looking at the texture of Toni Morrison's texts, you are doing the fable, a kind of dream memory, and Eleanor adopts the voice, the mode of the author that she's writing about, and I think that that is *so* respectful.

JT: I was interested in that in your talk you mentioned that you had worked on a screenplay for *Tar Baby*.[4]

TCB: I did the first draft for the screenplay for Toni Morrison's novel *Tar Baby*. She did the second draft, and I'm not sure who is going to be doing the third draft. But the movie is going into production this fall.

JT: Did she ask you to do the first draft or did you offer? How did you get involved in doing somebody else's work?

TCB: Originally the producer had a number of people in mind, Richard Wesley, Charles Fuller, a number of playwrights who were members of the screen-writers guild and had done work in Hollywood. A number of people he asked said that they were too soft, but there was a tough cookie in Atlanta named Toni Cade Bambara who was also a member of the screen-writers guild. Also there were people who were too busy, but a number of people recommended me, and so we finally met and talked and agreed on a deal.

JT: Back on *The Salt Eaters*, you seemed to be very concerned with the idea of "wholeness," and I relate you there to Alice Walker, and you are also very tied up with "the mud mothers" which I relate to Toni Morrison's "ancient properties." You all seem to be moving in the same general direction. Do you identify with what critics are calling the "Black Women's Renaissance"? Do you feel that you all have common touchstones?

TCB: Out of the maybe 120 black women writers that get coverage—and that's a small portion of the ones that are producing work in the major press industry and the small press industry as well as a small press community that people are calling now a subculture for reasons unbeknownst to me—but out of that group we all certainly derive from a similar tradition; we are all aware of a chorus or a community of voices. We certainly all read each other, we all know each other, some of us grew up together, some of us are friends, some of us talk on the phone, we might travel together in delegations, we might meet each other on the reading and speaking circuit. So we're not unfamiliar with each other. We share ideas, we frequently tip our hats to each other in the texts. So there are certainly some connections, and, too, there are just certain kinds of ideas that are in the air because it's the moment. For example, black women's health, the whole issue that constitutes health. Since the sixties there has been rather widespread organizing, particularly in the South, of health collectives by black women, like Lily Avery did in Atlanta with the National Black Women's Project, which now has three or four dozen chapters, or such as the Southern Rural Network of Black Women, which has a very strong health component. The health issue is crucial, and also there has been a lot of work done reviving the importance of midwifery in the homes. A woman named Linda Holms, a marvelous organizer, journalist, and poet has been doing a project for about two years now working in Alabama, primarily New Jersey, but all over the place, setting up conferences with midwives, trying to collect that history, trying to put that oral history together. So it's one of those things that's in the air. All of us are involved in some way or another in some kind of organizing around heath, so it's not odd that you might find any number of books coming out with the same type of stories that tend to hit at that question.

JT: When I was in France in April, I had the opportunity to listen to Toni Morrison, whom I greatly enjoyed.
TCB: She's special.

JT: Well, I think all of you are. But I asked her about something that she had said in an interview to the effect that the greatest differences that she can see today are between white women writers and black women writers, and I asked her why she thought so. Her answer was that white men write about white men, white women write about their problems with white men, black men write about their confrontation with white men, but black women write about each other. Do you see that? Do you feel that's true? Is it true for you?

TCB: I think it's a solid answer; it's a precise observation in general. In my own work I write about community.

JT: But you write from a woman's perspective very definitely. For example, the end of *The Salt Eaters*, which is tremendously complicated, the woman's perspective . . .

TCB: Is always primary, unless, of course, I'm writing a story from a male's point of view such as "The Tender Man."

JT: Well, that's part of what I meant about your versatility. You slip in and out of roles so easily.

TCB: It's called writing. [Unfortunately the transcript cannot reproduce the delightfully warm laughter that accompanied this remark.]

JT: But not all writers do it as well, is my comment. Do you feel that you are honest when you write from the male's point of view? Can you understand the male?

TCB: They're not mysterious.

JT: Do you think women are?

TCB: No. Well, yes, but there's a difference between genuine mystery and mere mystification. It's all a mystery finally, but I think the degree to which you are removed from power is the degree to which you are very sharp in your observations of other people, because it's a matter of life and death. Black people understand white people more than white people understand black people because we have to. Women understand men greater than men need be attentive to women because we have to. To that extent, I think, looking at any books at random, the portraits of men done by women seem to me more solid and more trustworthy than the portraits of women done by men.

JT: You sound very close to what Alice Walker says: It's just a question of who has been looking at whom for the longest time. Also as I mentioned before, your preoccupation with "wholeness" of the person, of the community, relates you very closely to Alice Walker . . .

TCB: With any black writer.

JT: But you specifically use the word "wholeness," is what I'm saying. You use it several times in *The Salt Eaters* with reference to Velma, Palma, Obie, Minnie, Old Wife, etc.

TCB: Yes, it's a nature motif.

JT: Do you know what you are looking for when you talk about wholeness? Do you have a very concrete idea of what it means to be whole?

TCB: What it means to have integrity? To have honor, to have health, to have responsibility, yes.

JT: When you wrote your essay for Mari Evans's book, *Black Women Writers (1950–1980): A Critical Evaluation*, entitled "Salvation Is the Issue,"[5] you said, "Laughter frequently glazes over the seams of the casing and cliché rage all but seals the very casing I would split and rip off to get at the inner works, to that underlying design that throws open the path to the new age, the new order in which I envision myself blowing a chorus or two in the language of the birth canal and maybe even of the caul." That is, you are looking for a new way of writing, of expression, and I assume that is what you are trying to do in *The Salt Eaters* . . .

TCB: No. I'm looking at some of the writers who are coming along now, particularly women who have done a lot of traveling, who may have linguistic backgrounds, and who come at the tradition from another angle. It's not that they are concerned so much with originality as with renewing the tradition, but they've got something else. There's something new that's happening because they belong to a generation that came of age after desegregation. So for so many years, freedom and protest literature, the protest voice was the key voice. And then a generation rose up where that's no longer the major issue, not that anything's been solved, but that is no longer the theme, and they are doing something else. And I think what they are doing is leading us past or leading us through this last quarter of the twentieth century to something that's up ahead. We don't have a vocabulary for talking about it yet, but I'm very aware in reading particularly some of the new young poets that are around the South that they're after another vision; they're after something new, something particular. They're bringing something down the canal.

JT: Do they know what they're doing? Or are they just looking?

TCB: I don't know; that's the last question in the world I would raise with a writer, "Do you know what you are doing?" meaning that the text is the answer, and if it's not there, the question is not meaningful. That is to say, when you have the text, there are several ways to evaluate its significance whether you're a critic or a reader: its value to the reader, its value to the moment, its value to history . . . and also its value to the artist at the moment of creation. As a reader, I'm struck by that first, and talking about these young poets coming up, there is something about the process of their having done this that is the answer to that question. It's a quest, it's a search, and the text is the question and the search and the answer. Another way to evaluate the significance, and it's really hard, is to evaluate the relationship of the text to itself.

JT: You are talking about process then. The process is the answer not the product. That's a very woman-oriented sort of evaluation.

TCB: That's the Black Aesthetic. The proposition of music is also about the process not the product. It's not going to be the same. We do "Body and Soul" this morning and then Coleman Hawkins does it tomorrow afternoon, it's not going to be the same. Even if we have the sheet music and the notations, it's not going to be the same. I can't get at this business of evaluating the text in terms of itself except to say that the story, or the situation, or the thing exists somewhere in the sound barrier, in the ether, I don't know, and it confronts you, beckons you, come and tell my story and you either shy away or you go ahead and do it. So, when people say, for example, what is your first concern when you're writing or having finished writing, the audience? the readership? No, your first concern is the story's relationship to itself: did you get it right? And it's almost not your relation to it, but is this the shadow story that came to you and did you get it right? Do those characters sort of nod; does the language sort of sparkle?

JT: The language is definitely impressive in *The Salt Eaters*. The first time I read the novel, to be honest, I plowed through it. I said to myself, "I am going to read *this book*" and I read *that book*. Once finished I found that I was glad that I had read *that book*. Yet a year later, a whole year of study later, I pick up the book and I find it delightful.

TCB: That's a typical experience. After the first version of Eleanor Traylor's critical discussion of *The Salt Eaters*, called "My Soul Looks Back in Wonder," which was published in the *First World*, I went and sat down and read the book again. Every time I read it, it is an act of discovery, but I particularly enjoyed it once she had organized that discussion around it.

JT: Oh, really? You mean you get things back from the critic?
TCB: Sure, that's what a good critic does. A good critic feeds it back to you and tells you how it's read, tells you how it is threaded, how they thread and read it. Then you can go back to it. Because you are not consciously thinking, "I will now set up a scene that does this and that . . ."

JT: It is very complicated. I read it and admired you all the way through it, but I swear it was difficult! It was much better after I read Gloria T. Hull's discussion,[6] who tried to divide it up a little bit and made more sense of the relationship of characters in it.
TCB: Both of those discussions together make a lot of sense: the notion of structuring a piece like a jazz suite, five tone scale, I mean, that device is very shrewd, very helpful; and then, Gloria's look at the circles which, of course, is really how it's put together.

JT: Is this very helpful?
TCB: It allows me to read it again in a new way.

JT: When Gloria Hull says correctly that you deal with everything in that book, and I think that practically every sociopolitical movement is mentioned in it, and you bring so many concerns of activists on all levels into it, she criticizes you for not bringing in anything about the gay movement.
TCB: It's a very accurate criticism, very sound.

JT: You take that as helpful?
TCB: Certainly, she's absolutely right.

JT: You were unaware of this, then? This omission was not on purpose? This was not something you don't want to touch?
TCB: No, I was not aware of its having not been there. And I'm even more amazed that it was not there since I'm very much part of the gay movement in the sense that I'm very supportive of what they're doing; in the sense that they bring to the whole question of how many frameworks and how many perspectives do we need in order to understand how this stuff is put together in order to dismantle it. I don't know of anything that's more important than the feminist analysis and the gay analysis, because you can be

as clear as you want about race and class, but you will not have it, you will not have all the prongs together. Once you get the sex-gender-caste pathologies, you're a lot clearer, because the class thing gets a lot clearer. Then once you get sexual preference, or the gay politic analysis, then you're really a lot clearer. And when I say I'm very much involved, I mean I don't know anybody that's keeping a closer watch, particularly on what lesbian critics are doing with texts, because I think they have a greater vested interest, a greater perspective, a more trustworthy perspective of the whole patriarchal oppression. And I think also they have a greater vested interest in dismantling it, in which case they have a lot to teach, and I very much pay attention to it. So the fact that I left it out is amazing to me.

JT: I admire your openness. You know you might have been defensive about the whole thing.
TCB: Oh, no, I'm very serious about improving. It feels good.

JT: I very much enjoyed your anthology *The Black Woman*,[7] read it cover to cover, but after all, that was compiled fifteen years ago. Have those concerns changed? Do you see that black women are still concerned about the same things? They must be somewhat since the book is now in its eighteenth edition.
TCB: I'm very concerned. As the editor, I am, of course, pleased that the book is moving and the royalties are still coming in, but as a member of the community, I'm alarmed, because that book by now should just be considered an interesting historical curiosity—"Oh, yes, things started, doors opened because of this book, there was a market out there"—and fine, and that should be the end of that discussion. The fact that it is still used and is still startling in some quarters is very scary. I really have not looked at that book in years so I really can't get too specific, but the book that I had meant to do, I may still do yet because no one has quite done it. And that was that originally I had wanted to pull together position papers on various women's groups, such as the women's caucus within the Black Panther Party for Self-Defense, the Third World Women's Alliances position papers, those of the women of SNCC, and so forth. That was the kind of book I originally wanted to do. There were lots of reasons mitigated against it, but I think it's extremely important now for someone to pull those old position papers together, as well as new things, things that are coming out of the Southern Rural Network, for example, out of the National Coalition of Women of Color. There's a massive organizing effort, broad-based organizing, going on now

and someone needs to start pulling those papers together. The concerns have not changed. No. Racism is still a problem, sexism is still a problem. We're still at the bottom: 75 percent of us are still in poverty; our children are still growing up in poverty; those kinds of issues are fairly chronic.

JT: You write at the beginning of the issue of *Southern Exposure* entitled "Southern Black Utterances Today," of which you were Special Issue Editor, that "Blk riting is not always and only about writing. Frequently it's about flexin, clenchin, arresting mad underdevelopers. Sometimes it's smothered incense."[8]

TCB: I think I was trying to demystify the notion of literature [this last word pronounced with a heavy, false British accent], the notion that when people produce a magazine, the first question is, is it a literary magazine? And you try to get a little bit clear about that because that makes you eligible for funding. If it's a literary magazine, then you can get literary funding. But the question arises, "Who's defining what as what? Or who has the right to define, who has the privilege?" I think in that statement at the beginning of the magazine I was simply trying to cut through that notion, because many people that we approached, certainly people that I approached—I co-edited that with Leah Wise—felt that they were not writers. You know, it's very hard to say "a writer is a person who writes," if the image of "writer" is somebody who runs around with cashmere sweaters and an Irish setter and a secretary. Somehow there is this image of the writer. So many people who had really fine stuff that I wanted and I felt belonged in there had to be told that "writing is when you say so and so and you put it down on paper; that's writing and you are a writer." And the statement was also addressed to lots of people who would pick up the magazine and expect to see the names that they generally associate with journals of literature.

JT: Do you define yourself that way? Are you a "literary person"?
TCB: In my neighborhood, particularly when I lived in Atlanta, people identified me as a writer, and they would come over to the house and say, "Well, what all do you write?" And I'd say, "Well, I write poems, and essays . . ." And they'd say, "Well, do you write protest letters?" "Yes, I do." "Can you go down to the corner to Miss Margaret's and help her write a letter to her nephew?" "Yes, I can." A writer is a writer. And they would pay me, and bring by Jell-o, fix my car, or shingle my roof, and I was the neighborhood writer. You want to sell your Ford wrecker? Fine, and I would write the contract. Give me a piece of paper and a pencil. That's what a writer does: a writer writes.

JT: You became known as a writer first as a short story writer, and you have said that you really enjoy the short form, even though it is not very orthodox to say so. You are now involved in writing another novel, but will you go back to the short story?

TCB: I'm always writing short stories. I like the form, I like the size, I like the fact that it makes a modest appeal for attention. There's no big fanfare. It's just a little story, so you can do a lot of things, you can get a lot of things done. I also like the short story because there's a very particular readership that won't hang with a novel but they'll read a short story. Most of the feedback, the most voluminous feedback that I get from readers is whenever a story appears in *Redbook*. I get all these letters commenting on the story, so I really do like that form and I stick with it.

JT: Are you compiling a new collection, or do you just keep writing until you feel that it's ready to go?

TCB: There are some stories that will go out some time this winter to journals, to magazines . . . There are times when you've written yourself out of the novel and you need time to let things percolate. Some people then choose to sit around and gnaw their fingernails and call it writer's block and go see the therapist. I prefer to simply change tables and work on something else. If someone calls up and says, "Well, we've got a new issue of so and so, do you have any stories?" I like to have one ready. So then I'll start working on the story and the novel or the script or whatever waits. However, if I'm working on a script, that tends to be all-consuming because TV and movie people want it right away, so that becomes a steady kind of work. But I'm always working on something. In fact, most writers I know are always working on any number of things for the simple reason that you have to.

JT: In your essay "Salvation Is the Issue" you state that while working on the TV film on the life and work of Zora Neale Hurston, you set up a four-by-eight-foot slab of sheetrock in the yard atop three sawhorses and worked out the scenes on butcher paper using different color pens. Did you actually write the script that way?

TCB: Yeah, and I really do recommend it. I ran a workshop not long ago with a number of writing students who had been absolutely locked, I mean the way your joints can get locked by terror, having taken course after course of writing courses, with maybe two or three teachers, and so they were constantly writing for these maybe two or three sensibilities, and they were just all locked up. They were absolutely in bondage in terms of rules—"You can't shift the point of view" and "You mustn't forget the relationship of time and place," and they were just bound up. So, we cleared the desk, and I brought in a bunch of butcher paper and we just brainstormed for a while, just walking around the room, just walking around the table, just writing. We decided to do something collaborative so we started an opera, or something, and everybody just wrote, and walked around the room and looked at what someone else wrote, and changed that scene.

There was a seduction scene that took place in an art gallery that I had set up and the woman's dialect was very hip, but I left the man's dialect kind of weak. So the men came over, and they'd straighten up that dialect and really fix it up. And it was wonderful, I mean, many people felt very much released. They found a new way to work. I highly recommend working on large pieces of paper anyway, if it's a large piece of work, because it's just hard to make the work manageable if you're doing a script or a novel. Some people work with three or four notebooks for the various chapters or the various versions. I just happen to like to see it all at once, so I like a large table with piece of paper. And in working on the Zora script, it seemed right to work outside.

JT: Has that been aired yet?
TCB: No, it was never finished.

JT: What happened to it?
TCB: Many of us were brand new at what we were doing; it was the first time the producer had produced, the director had directed, and the first time I had done a script, but it just got dropped, primarily because I got caught up in the Atlanta missing and murdered children situation because a girlfriend of ours was missing. So that got me off the project, and as I say when you work with media you have to give up all your time. You must keep checking in, people knock on your door, etc., and I could not keep up that pace, but it may come around again.

JT: You are now working on a script for a movie about the Senegalese, African Americans, and other blacks in the German concentration camps during World War II. Is that still in the works?
TCB: Yes. I've been wanting to do something for a long time about the numbers of black people who were lost in the camps. No one ever talks about it.

JT: I have never even read anything about it.

TCB: It's not a matter of reading. In the past seven years I have not found anything in print that I can use, I mean that speaks to me really. But I remember growing up, listening to folks (there were always meetings at my house) who had been in vaudeville in the thirties and wound up in Europe and got caught in France during the war, or people I know, my uncle for example, who had deliberately gone to Germany because he had a child there from World War I, and he got caught. If you go to Germany, of course, there are black people in Germany, there have been black people there since the eighteenth century. And they thought they were citizens, until the rise of the Nazi party, so they were all under house arrest, and were afraid to leave their homes. Many of them wound up in the camps and died. Lots of people, again vaudevillians from the States as well as black people in Hungary who were part of the traveling circuses, took refuge in Denmark, only through that embassy they and the diplomats got rounded up. So I'm doing two things on that; one is a book and one is a movie, and they don't have too much to do with each other. It's not the novelization of the movie or the movie version of a book; they're just two different kinds of projects. One is a movie that I intend to do some time this year, and the other is a novel that keeps nudging me up at night so I'm sure I'll get started on it sometime this month probably.

JT: Are you close to finishing your novel on the Atlanta missing and murdered children?
TCB: Yes. *If Blessing Comes* should go into copy production this spring and should be out next fall.

JT: Did you get started on this novel for personal reasons, as you said before that you had a friend who was missing?
TCB: No, I got involved in this because I am a community worker, and I work in the streets and I was very much aware that something was going on, and that attention was not being paid to it.

JT: Isn't it very hard for you to be so caught up in such an emotional issue and yet be objective enough to write a novel about it?
TCB: Well, I've never felt any obligation to be objective or even reasonable. What concerned me about the pain of doing that book was not being objective, or reasonable or even fair, was that I didn't want to produce a "chill-out," because that doesn't get anything done. And it was very hard because there were many people who actually betrayed the city, other friends

of mine, so that made it very difficult. The real agony of doing a book like that is that you have to stay with it, and that everyone must be taken into account, and I don't want to hustle anybody, which is one of the reasons it's a novel and not a documentary. Telling the truth in a country where there are no truth-speaking traditions that are respected is extremely hard.

JT: It's just that it's so recent, and people seem to find that some kind of distancing is needed to get it all in, to get it all together—though maybe that's the white-male-academic attitude—while you have been so close in to what was happening in Atlanta.

TCB: It requires somebody very close because the highly selective police-media fiction that has been accepted as the version of the truth can only be broken open by somebody who is very close. Atlanta is a very interesting town, as any town is; it's a wonderful place, that has a very heavy PR. Its image is extremely important, being the third busiest convention city in the country, and many people who have lived there all their lives, fifth and sixth generation Atlantans, otherwise very coherent, very intelligent, fall under the spell of the PR and will accept that version—I don't just mean of the case—they will accept any version of the city in spite of their own experience. That's very scary. But in some ways it's very peculiar to convention towns. For example, there was a time when Maynard Jackson, who was a very beloved mayor but isn't always under control, also began to believe the PR. And he spoke in Cleveland, Ohio, saying there were jobs, and boom prosperity and construction. People came by the droves into Atlanta with their suitcases, ready to move into the city! And it became a tremendous burden on the city hall workers, which of course was where they showed up, and all of it was based on this compelling talk that Maynard had done because he was under the spell of the PR! You know, this is getting kind of weird!

JT: Is Random House going to publish this novel also?
TCB: Yes, this will be a Ventures paperback.

JT: Did they just say, "Fine, go ahead and do it?"
TCB: The last contract I signed was a two-book contract.

JT: You have spoken of things, people disappearing, for example, SNCC being "written out" of the Civil Rights history, and I would think it would be in the interest of some people to "write out" or "disappear" your version of the

Atlanta missing and murdered case. Didn't you have any problems? Have you been pressured in any way at all?

TCB: A security question is raised, certainly. I'm not a crazy person, certainly. It's a dangerous business.

JT: Are you not afraid?

TCB: Well, yes, but playing safe doesn't make you safe; being quiet doesn't make you safe. Trying to play it safe makes you crazy.

[Interview conducted in New Orleans, Louisiana, in September 1985.]

Notes

1. Toni Cade Bambara, *The Salt Eaters* (London: The Women's Press, Ltd., 1982).

2. Toni Cade Bambara, *The Sea Birds Are Still Alive* (New York: Random House, 1982).

3. Eleanor W. Traylor, "Music as Theme: The Jazz Mode in the Works of Toni Cade Bambara," in *Black Women Writers (1950–1980): A Critical Introduction*, ed. Mari Evans (Garden City, New York: Anchor Press/Doubleday, 1984), pp. 58–70.

4. Toni Morrison, *Tar Baby* (London: Triad/Panther Books, 1984).

5. Bambara in Evans, pp. 41–47.

6. Gloria T. Hull, "What It Is I Think She's Doing Anyhow: A Reading of Toni Cade Bambara's *The Salt Eaters*," in *Home Girls: A Black Feminist Anthology*, ed. Barbara Smith (Kitchen Table: Women of Color Press, 1983), pp. 124–42.

7. Toni Cade Bambara, *The Black Woman: An Anthology* (New York and Scarborough, Ontario: New American Library, 1970).

8. *Southern Exposure: Southern Black Utterances Today*, Volume III, Number 1 (Spring/Summer, 1975), inside cover.

An Interview with Toni Cade Bambara

Zala Chandler/1987

Excerpted from "Voices beyond the Veil: An Interview with Toni Cade Bambara and Sonia Sanchez." From Joanne M. Braxton and Andrée Nicola McLaughlin, eds., *Wild Women in the Whirlwind: Afra-American Culture and the Contemporary Literary Renaissance.* Copyright © 1990 by Rutgers, The State University. Reprinted by permission of Rutgers University Press.

Chandler: Who are some of the women who have most influenced and in-spired your work?

Bambara: First, you must consider that I grew up in Harlem in the late thirties, forties, and fifties, at a time when the McCarthy period very much determined political style. It was a period of tremendous fear and paranoia, where people were surrendering up each other without even the threat of torture—in many ways comparable to this current period in which people comply with insanity and surrender up integrity without, again, even the threat of torture.

This period was also characterized by people's consciousness that Har-lem was, indeed, a wealthy community, a community where African genius was very much in evidence in individuals, organizations, and forums. One such forum that was very much in place was Speakers Corner, a street cor-ner where at any point in time, on any given day, we could hear women from the sanctified churches, women from the Ida B. Wells clubs, the Temple People (which is what we used to call the Muslims), the Abyssinians (which is what we used to call the Rastas), trade unionists, Party members, and members of the National Negro Congress. We also had the Apollo, lots of clubs, black bookstores, auditoriums such as that in the Harlem YMCA, and, of course, the Schomburg Library. Additionally, we had a number of theaters which would open up every now and then as community meeting places, for example, the Lafayette Theater.

When I think of women who have influenced me, several groups of women come to mind immediately. The tap dancers and the be-bop musicians of the forties, the Chitlin' Circuit women, the black slip mamas, the sanctified church women, the women of the Ida B. Wells clubs, and my mother.

The tap dancers and the be-bop musicians influenced the pitch and pace of my work. And along with the Chitlin' Circuit women, including women like Jackie "Moms" Mabley, they made me very curious about the national and international black community. You see, these were women who traveled a lot, and they would bring back information from all over the country and all over the world.

The black slip mamas were the women who had any number of kinds of jobs; however, they never defined themselves in terms of the work they did. They defined themselves, rather, in terms of what kinds of friends they were to each other. They would gather in various people's kitchens or bedrooms, pulling out the old hatbox and going over old dance programs, talking with each other and playing cards together. And they were always, somehow, walking around in black slips and smoking Lucky Strikes, Old Gold, Pall Mall, or some other filterless cigarette. They were concerned very much with race issues. They were race women in the sense that, like the Chitlin' Circuit and the be-bop women, they did a lot of traveling and they made use of their homes as hostels—a place where other women on the road were always free to stop for a hot meal, a warm bath, and a bed.

There were the beauty parlor women. These women were my first conscious heroines in the sense that not only did they do your hair—they did your head! We young girls would often hang around and eavesdrop on their conversations, not realizing that they were really conversing for our benefit. It is through these women that we learned standards of sexual behavior, sexual politics, and, most important, race issues. Besides being race women, these women also tended to be analysts of various neighborhood situations. If something was going on in the neighborhood, one could stop by the beauty parlor (or barber shop) to hear it laid out.

Another group of women who moved me were the sanctified church women, members of the Women's Departments of the various sanctified churches. These women frequently spoke on Speakers Corner. They were significant because they were the historians of the church, and, as such, they always ensured that the contributions of women in the church were "lifted up." They taught women how to be speakers, to be historians, to be researchers, to be bibliophiles, and they trained women to travel, to balance budgets, and to monitor each other's development.

The members of the Ida B. Wells Club were very important to me because they were historians and they were investigative journalists. They tended to be women with professional privilege who were very clear that their skills were important only when they were put forth in service for mass-class women.

Finally, in terms of individuals, I think that the most important inspiration was, of course, my mother, who was a combination of things beyond the usual "mothering." One, she kept sparkling bookcases and an interesting collection of books for us to read. Two, she had a tremendous respect for the mind—the activity of the mind and the privacy of imagination. My mother never interrupted either my brother or me if we were daydreaming. She recognized that as important work to do. Three, she became very interested and curious about what was going on in the museums and in the music and concert halls; she would drag us everywhere—not only for our benefit but for her benefit as well. And fourth, she had a tremendous sense of justice and injustice. I don't think that she would describe herself as a very fierce or courageous person, but she would always stand up on issues. She reminds me of Ms. Rosa Parks in that way. I think of my mother as very much like that—a very quiet person, not inclined to jump up about issues—certainly not inclined to consider herself a leader. Nonetheless, for a great many people my mother was certainly the first, the paramount, and the ultimate, inspirational woman.

Chandler: What about women in the literary tradition?
Bambara: Well, ignoring the barrier that we usually erect between "literature" and other kinds of writing, I would say Ida B. Wells and Harriet Tubman. I am drawn temperamentally toward "pistol packing mamas," so from a very early age right up until this moment, they have always been models for me. Their courage, their absolute unwillingness to engage in the politics of silence and the politics of invisibility and amnesia has always inspired me.

Harriet Tubman, as we all know, defied all obstacles, including the threat of death, to make a difference. Ida B. Wells, as a journalist, an organizer, and as a gadfly, was a person who would needle people into correct positions. She would browbeat people, embarrass people into taking radical positions. To me, she is and always has been a model of what a writer is supposed to be about—namely to take very bold positions and not hide behind camouflaged language. In essence, Ida B. Wells recognized that writing is simply one way to get the work done, but organizing is really what it is about.

Chandler: Can you discuss some of the spiritual and political forces at work in your life, your writings?

Bambara: Through time, I've come to realize that, for many people, there is a division between the religious or the sacred and the secular. For me it is all sacred. I've become recently aware, however, that there need to be statements made about the spiritual and the political . . . the need for the two to join hands.

One of the concerns that led me into the novel *The Salt Eaters* was pretense. I had a "grandmother" (not blood kin but spirit kin) who had a little statement that would just knock me out. I would come bustling over to her place with all kinds of questions and issues and so forth and so on. And grandma would just look at me and ask, "What are we *pretending* not to know today?" The premise being that colored people on the planet earth really know everything there is to know. And if one is not coming to grips with the knowledge, it must mean that one is either scared or pretending to be stupid.

One of the ways that we pretend (and it is easy to do so because we are rewarded for pretense) is to act as though we live in a logical, rational, "two plus two equals four" setup. Yet reality is also psychic. That is to say, in addition to all the other things, for example, the political, we live in a system that is guided by a spiritual order. Now, there is a Western bias against this kind of thinking that goes back in this country to the Pilgrims. Those astringent Pilgrims who arrived in the New World with what they considered a more perfect way to worship, took one look at the "unruly" bunch that met them at the shore, the hospitality committee, and called them savages. (This was the beginning of "disconnectedness" as an American disease.) And they proceeded to ban the drum, ban smoke signals, and ban what they called fetish religions. In its place, they would impose a system of logic on the American psyche, the American sensibility, the American political reality, and, indeed, American life and literature that was aimed all the while at a total control of society by a few.

The unwillingness of the cultural brokers and powerbrokers of this society to acknowledge smoke signals, the drum, or the existence of intelligence channels other than their rationality and logic results in a language, namely English, that does not accommodate discussion of those phenomena outside of the Western logic. English is a wonderful mercantile language. You can get a lot of trade done with English. But you would find it very difficult to validate the psychic and spiritual existence of your life. Consequently, we pretend. We pretend that we're not clairvoyant, and we buy glasses instead.

We pretend that we're not telepathic, and we lean on the telephone and post office system instead, etc. As a result, those of us who are adept, who have dormant powers, have to expend a great deal of time and energy denying it and suppressing it—to the detriment of the individual and the entire community.

What compelled me to tackle all of that in *Salt* was the amount of psychic and spiritual damage that is being done to us, and the fact that we're encouraged to either ignore or laugh at the damage. The novel opens with what seems to be a very simple question, "Do we want to be well?" The answer tends to be "no!" To be *whole*—politically, psychically, spiritually, culturally, intellectually, aesthetically, physically, and economically whole—is of profound significance. It is significant because there is a correlative to this. There is a responsibility to self and to history that is developed once you are "whole," once you are well, once you acknowledge your powers.

Additionally, I know that we must reclaim those bones in the Atlantic Ocean. Do you know that there is not a plaque, a memorial, a day, a ritual, or an hour that is erected in memorial to those one hundred million bodies in the Atlantic Ocean? All those African bones in the briny deep. All those people who said "no" and jumped ship. All those people who tried to figure out a way to steer, to navigate amongst the sharks. We don't call upon that power. We don't call upon those spirits. We don't celebrate those ancestors. We don't have a marker, an expression, a song that we all use to acknowledge them. We have nothing to indicate that those are our people and they matter! We willingly embrace amnesia and willingly self-administer knockout drops. More horrendous is the fact that we have all that power that we don't tap; we don't tap into the ancestral presence in those waters.

Chandler: Does spirituality actually play a role in compelling you to work?
Bambara: I work every day, all the time, because it is a compulsion. It is also because there is much for us to consider—there's so much unhealth and just rampant bullshit to counter that every day I know of yet another reason to set the alarm clock one hour earlier. And like most writers I know, most cultural workers I know, and most especially, most black women I know, I always have ten or fifteen projects cooking because I never know which one is going to fly first or which one is going to get past that bend in the tunnel where the light is stuck.

In terms of that psychic engine that frequently drives a work, there are times when I put my work aside. That is to say that I just don't feel fit to work on it. I'll go and do something else. But spirit will call me back. For example,

I have been working for the past six years on a novel based on the missing and murdered children's case in Atlanta. There were times while I was living in Atlanta when the work was simply too horrendous, when the amount of treachery . . . and betrayal . . . and viciousness . . . and lack of heart was simply too dispiriting for me to pick myself up and return to the work table. And I would take what I call a "vacation." I would go to the local bar, only to find that the conversation next to me was something about the case. I would hear something that either confirmed what I was thinking or reconstructing regarding the children, or I gained some brand new information. One time I went to the airport to take a plane to do a gig in Houston, and I found the police commissioner on line trying to sneak out of Atlanta to go and take a new job. Or I would go to the library, attempting to do some research on yet another project, and I would find myself sitting next to a sister who worked in the SAFE office downtown. She would be talking to the person sitting next to her and telling her all that she had experienced with the safety education projects. Or I would take time off and simply try to take a walk in the woods, and I would run into a command unit of "Survivalists" who would be talking about how to capture control of Civilian Search Teams that had been put together by the United Youth and Adult Conference. Or I would be driving with plans to totally get away from the killing ground, and I would go to a restaurant in another county, only to hear at the table behind me a journalist interviewing someone from the Task Force—in spite of the gag order. And I would again be confronted with information that either confirmed the version that I had constructed in my head as a result of my research, my instinct, and my knowledge of our history, or I would receive new information. Do you see the pattern? I was not allowed to leave that case alone.

My "grandmother" used to say that if you're doing what you're supposed to be doing, then the whole universe will accommodate itself to you. That is to say, if you are on the right track, and you are committed, and your intentions are clear, then you can be passive because the information you need, the teachers you need, the people you need, the resources you need are going to come towards you. And all you have to do is be receptive.

While working on that novel, there was a period of approximately nine months in which I never left the house. I would get up in the morning, go straight downstairs, hop in the big leather chair, and begin shuffling the index note cards while trying to decide if the version I had in my head could possibly be correct. The phone would ring, and it might be someone from one of the major television networks or a movie production company that had come to town in search of the story. They called me, I guess, because

I'm a black woman, a writer, a community worker, and I happened to be in the phone book. And when they asked me for an angle, I would look at one of my index cards and send them in search of a particular clue. They would call me back, giving me the information, information they would say that they couldn't use because it had nothing to do with the "official" version. So for nine months, I had a squad of researchers who I did not have to pay and who were working diligently on my behalf without knowing it. I never had to leave my chair. "Grandma" was right! Once you understand what your work is and you do not try to avert your eyes from it, but attempt to invest energy in getting that work done, the universe will send you what you need. You simply have to know how to be still and receive it.

I think that even if I were not a writer, I would have been compelled to become a writer in order to document what was going on in Atlanta. I felt an obligation to provide a forum for the version that was so different from the official one.

Chandler: Can you please talk a little about what you see as the role and responsibility of black women writers today.
Bambara: At this stage in life, I try not to comment on what people ought to be doing. It is enough that I can get clear about what I'm supposed to be doing! But I will tell you what my main thrust has been as an educator, and I will comment on what I think *is being done* by black women writers today.

As a teacher, my main thrust in the classroom has always been to encourage and equip people to respect their rage and their power. To not back off from what you know to be the case. To understand that your own experiences and knowledge of history make you an expert in regard to certain questions, namely the black agenda. By the black agenda, of course, I mean answering questions like: what are our prospects, what are the realities of our condition, and where are our arenas of power?

One of the greatest afflictions in American society for both the teacher/ student and the writer is the affliction of disconnectedness. The separation between the world of academia and the world of knowledge that exists beyond the campus gates, the seeming dichotomy between politics and ethics, the division between politics and art, the division between dead authors and live authors, etc., etc. It is extremely difficult to arrive at the formula for living or for defining what the black agenda should be, once you fall victim to this disconnectedness. In this society, forgetfulness is a virtue, amnesia is a virtue. We are always asked to celebrate the new and improved laundry detergent as though that which came out yesterday is already obsolete. And we carry this habit, this outlook, into our daily lives. This is extremely dangerous. So I teach about the necessity of being connected, and about the necessity of resurrecting the truth about our experiences (and revising the texts) in this place called America.

Three things seem to be going on with the writings of black women today. One, there is a kind of book and film that is coming out which deals with the experiences of African Americans in Africa. Most of these books and documents tend to look back at the sixties and seventies at African Americans in places like Tanzania, Kenya, Ghana, and Nigeria, especially. They tend to be about the collision of two African cultures—New World and Old World. Martina Golden's *Migrations of the Heart* is but one of about fifteen books that I can think of that attempts to look at, to put its finger on, moments of collision between the African American set of assumptions and the African set of assumptions in the twentieth century.

The second type of book that black women tend to be producing has to do with our sense of community. Unlike the protest writers of the forties and fifties, the new writers see oppression as a temporary reality. They see the community as the paramount reality, the permanent, eternally valid reality. Consequently, we get books about relationships, about supportive networks. We get books that investigate cultural mores and habits that speak to health, that speak to friendship, and that speak to mutual support. Of course, there is a tradition for this; we have Zora Neale Hurston who provided us with novels of cultural maintenance. Zora Neale was attempting to acknowledge, document, and celebrate the folk tradition—and also to look at ways in which it is useful. (And she caught hell for this.) I think that the women writers who are coming along now—especially the younger sisters out of the South—are tending to take that a step further, namely to look at our culture with a critical eye, determining what is useful and what is reactionary. That which is found to be reactionary is then critiqued, and that which is found to be progressive is celebrated. This is the healthiest strain of writing today.

The third kind of writing tends to be very personal, but in my mind the writers are still part of the collective because connections are made. Many people get impatient with that kind of work because it is so "I," "I," "I" or "me," "me," "me." But I think that the works that come after this will be more consciously collective. When I look at the seeming personal autobiographies written in novel form in 1986, they tend to hark back to that Linda Brent kind of slave narrative, where there is tremendous concern for an individual black woman with a particular set of experiences. But I think that in the long run they are leading toward presenting an understanding that many of these experiences are not peculiar to the individual, are not symptomatic of some type of personal deficit, but rather are part and parcel of a whole oppressive machinery, engineered against people because they are black, because they are women, because they are working class, etc. So I think that the novels that come after this will be more intentionally, willfully collective in spirit and, like Zora's, communal in perspective.

Chandler: Can you comment on the various movements of black people in recent history, for example, the Civil Rights Movement, the Black Power Movement; and can you attempt to define the period in which we currently exist?

Bambara: We're in the twelfth year of the last quarter of the twentieth century. And the two major issues domestically and internationally are one, the development of an independent black political party with a sound agenda for our survival and development as a people, and two, the South Africa question. Surrounding the question of South Africa, the reality is that campus and youth forces—particularly black people—have not skipped a beat. Students are still adamant on the divestment question. There are still demonstrations, rallies, teach-ins, and sit-ins.

One of the things that continues to set us back is this huge land mass in the United States. Unless we're traveling around a lot, we do not make certain kinds of connections. We can get disillusioned and think that nothing is going on. The media "white out" makes an activist group in one area, unaware of other concerted actions, feel isolated and singular.

One of the reasons that I guess I do not have a "job" is because there is a lot of traveling that has to be done, and somebody has to do it. I move from campus to campus, community center to community center, and organization to organization in the Southwest, the Northeast, and on the West Coast in search of patterns. The patterns show me that we are organizing—cell by cell, block by block, city by city. Clearly, one of the patterns is a move against South Africa and support for the freedom-fighting forces there. Another is a growing coalition amongst homeless people making demands upon cities and states. And still another is an increased move against state violence, i.e., police brutality.

But all of this speaks to the fact that we need an independent black political party that would have the ability to coordinate these efforts and be able to fashion both domestic and foreign policies, not to mention establish a comprehensive information network of the independent video makers, film makers, radio stations, and press. It is important that we give enough support to our cultural workers so that certain kinds of information can be packaged in different kinds of ways and spread from East Coast to West Coast, from North to South. If we have learned anything from the fifties and sixties, it is that we need an organized, collective response to our oppression.

Chandler: Are you optimistic about our future?
Bambara: I am always optimistic. Sometimes angry. Concerned. Questioning. Eager for us to resurrect the fighters and the builders who have come before us. Eager for us to see all the connections, the ties that bind us to one another. Eternally optimistic.

A Conversation
with Toni Cade Bambara

Akasha (Gloria) Hull/1987

Transcribed tape recording from the San Francisco State University Video Collection. Previously unpublished. Printed by permission of Akasha (Gloria) Hull.

Akasha (Gloria) Hull: I guess the first thing I want to say is I am glad to be sitting here. I don't know that there have been many occasions where somebody has decided to place a writer and a critic on stage and say have a dialogue. When I saw that, at first, I did not know what that sort of thing would look like. But then it made all the sense in the world to me because—I have said this to a couple of people in private, but now I am going to say it in public—I believe that Toni's work in the world is to write what she writes and I believe that my work in the world is to read it and to help other people read it too. So that is what sitting up here is all about, and it feels good to me.

I am also sitting here doing what a lot of us in the audience were doing as we listened to that excerpt of "Till Blessings Come" [*Those Bones Are Not My Child*]. We were moved by it because it was so powerful. I was also trying to figure out what comes before, what comes after, kind of getting a little bit of Sundiata's story and trying to piece it out from the little that was there. But also like those of us who have read *The Salt Eaters* and other Toni Cade Bambara works, I was feeling the ways that it felt familiar and also thinking: is this you [the writer]? I remember once, before Toni Morrison's *Beloved* came out, I asked her: "When we read this, will we know it's you?" And so part of what I was doing, Toni, was looking for the "youness" that's in there. And I think for me the first thing that came was, "Yes, this woman who says of herself that she is an elaborator by nature who pulls out all the verbal stops, is certainly doing that in this particular book." It reminded me, for instance, of the moments in *The Salt Eaters* when everything sort of stopped action at a particular point and you do what I note in the margins of my book. I call it the milk-the-moment technique *[laughter from audience]* where everything that you could possibly get out of a moment is done such that it really resonates. I mean all of what was going on between Sundiata and Mamma Lovey, I mean all the dialectics of that relationship which went backward and forward. In fact, it just really reminds me of, say, the whole structure of *Salt* where what's happening takes in everything at once. So I'm sitting here saying, "Yes, I can see all that," and trying to figure that out, really trying to work through it.

[Long uncomfortable pause between Hull and Bambara, as Bambara waits for Hull's question. Audience and discussants laugh at this.]

Toni Cade Bambara: *[Pauses for a long time. She smiles.]* Yes. *[Continues to smile and Hull laughs again]* Yeah.

AGH: Okay, I can talk some more and turn it into a question. *[Both laugh again]*
TCB: Okay.

AGH: Alright. The other thing I was thinking was the whole question of, well, two things: form and language. But I'll start with the form. I read a head note in *Race and Class*, which published a little excerpt from the novel [*Those Bones*]. They said it was cast partly in fictional form. And it also used journals. I know you do use journals a lot (also in teaching a course called the writer's journal) and I realize that this book is also what you could call fact-based fiction. I was listening to what you had to say about how it started off as fiction, but the more things came up it's looking like documentary. And I realize that it is indeed documentary, a little bit of exposé journalism. It made me think about the whole general question of the way that contemporary black women writers are finding traditional notions of form and genre very inadequate—to say the least—and in fact, finding these traditional notions very unworkable. I am also thinking about form for you and just your own particular ways of trying to negotiate that. In Jamaica they have a phrase where they talk about people being broad with nothing about them being little. You are like really, really broad. The short story is something you like; you say that it is your druthers. You also do film. I am wondering how would you place *Blessings* in terms of form, or if that even feels like an issue?
TCB: It's strange because it required a lot of work. That is to say in the be-

ginning, in 1979, 1980, when we were aware that something very strange was going on in the black community, a number of murders and abductions of men, women, and children, I was writing entries in my journal. Then there was a period when we were putting out newsletters ("we" meaning a sort of miscellaneous collection of community workers). We began putting out newsletters because the police weren't. I mean people felt very vulnerable and angry and real crazy when they learned a week later that a week before there had been three murders and two abductions around the corner and nobody had informed them. So we began putting out newsletters. But we did not have a lot of money, so the challenge was trying to get a lot of information in a little bit of space. We also had to package information so that it is not "ah, ah" *[she mocks making inaudible sounds or someone making useless words]*. So many of us had to learn how to write little haikus. Our thought was pictures with captions in an attempt to try to get it out. And there was a time when, every once in a while we might get some space in a newspaper. The newspaper might call me up and say, "We know your work very well. We love your poems. *[Bambara pauses, rolls her eyes and the audience laughs]* And we would like to give you some space." Right. "A page." Right. So then I would write some poems about the situation in Atlanta. The message or information required ways to communicate with the community taking many forms. Many of us would use many forms to do that: graffiti on the walls, fliers, leaflets, you know, anything. You can think of a poem, great, give me some space to write a poem.

And I had five or six great little poems that had to do with how the community was being affected by being under siege. Then there were longer journalistic pieces and narrative essays and stuff. It was quite a while before I realized that that narrative essay that appeared in *Race and Class* was indeed the beginning of a book, the prologue of a book. The book has been a marriage of fictional impulse, documentary impulse, investigative journalism, detective mystery genre of writing. A little of this, a little of that—it has been crazy. But what I think has emerged. . . .

AGH: Have you coined the word that puts it all together? I remember Audre Lorde developed the term *biomythography*. *[Laughter from audience]*
TCB: No. It's a novel. I kept a lot of notes on my process, blending this and that because I knew there might be a moment when someone might ask me to be intelligent about it. Any writers out there? *[She directs her question to the audience.]* Come on, a writer is a person who writes. I talk about it only because, there is always one of those difficult questions when you are sort of

playing around with what it is, whatever it is, hoping you will keep writing, you will write your way there, and hoping that the form or shape will appear. And that it will emerge and it will announce itself and you'll say, "Hey okay . . . Time." *[Laughter from audience]*

And then you can work with it, but this thing, you know, every time the question is, what is this? What kind of thing is this?

After a while a number of the community workers were actually dogged about not going to sleep, not embracing amnesia, not going to the doctor. So, a lot of information had been suppressed and destroyed from '81 to '86. Now, the book reads very much as though I had been on some secret investigations, which means I have to now write something about that because my argument is kind of: If I can sit down in my house and be quiet and still, operating with nothing more than the history of what it means for us to be in this fight, and I can reconstruct what happened, then surely professional investigators with $8 million—it was an $8 million investigation, dah, dah, dah, dah, dah . . .

AGH: Yeah.

TCB: . . . and with computers and dah, dah, dah, you know, you could [meaning the government authorities], you know, do it. But, also, another argument being: Well, if I can sit down in my chair, because that is what grandma says, "be still" and pull together what actually happened, it means also that this question that we keep raising throughout the African diaspora: "When are we gonna put together international commissions of inquiry?" [It] can happen. But it doesn't really require, you know, a whole lot of funds and a whole lot of resources and a whole lot of, you know, a really great intelligence to know that we are being killed. In fact, whenever we hear that we always know; that Monday, October 12, 13, 1981, when this nursery blew up in Atlanta we first started hearing about the case. Every black person in this room knew. Just as you knew in November of 1978, and we saw 911 bodies face down in the jungles of Guyana. We knew.

AGH: We knew.

TCB: Just as Mother's Day, 1985, when you heard the news commentator say in the morning, "The police are having a confrontation with militants," meaning black people, and then by afternoon that confrontation was "stepping up with the radicals," you know?

AGH: Right.

TCB: And then by evening, and slowly, you know, the police are having this thing with the "extremists," meaning mad dog hatred was about to be unleashed. We always know, but we wait until we get the official word; so then we can crack on it. It's our cynical style or something, but what we really need is an international commission.

AGH: Actually, that sounds like kind of what you're doing.
TCB: Pardon?

AGH: Sounds like part of what you're doing in *If Blessing Comes* is what you always do. I think that's why you're so special. You make us know the things that we don't want to know. It's to make us confront the things that it's easier not to confront. When you start off *The Salt Eaters* with a question, which we talked a little bit about in the workshop: "Are you sure, sweetheart, that you want to be well?" Sounds a little bit like when we read the new book, it will be a question of another kind. Well, a question of the same kind, another rhetoric, another key is all. Do we—are we ready to know what that book is about? Would that be a kind of fair thing to say?
TCB: Mmmm hmmm.

AGH: Is it gonna tell it to us, you know? How will it confront us in that same kind of way, that question "Are you sure you want to be well?" does?
TCB: I don't know. All I'm asking, essentially, is do we understand what it means when you buy into the official version of things? I mean, we know why we do it because it's easier. To be responsible for your eyes or be responsible for what you hear, what you know, it takes a lot of energy, a lot of courage. In so many ways it seems easier to wait for that phony, bogus, official version, even though you know damn well that it's not being composed in our interest. At least it gives us something to gripe about.

AGH: Well, I think it's something that addicts you too.
TCB: I think it's a funny addiction too; the addiction to official versions; to spend life pushing up against 'em and reacting to them. I know many people who are addicted. Can't wait for the official version to come out so they can say *[sucks her teeth and turns her head]* something.

AGH: And that is like a dismissing of it at the same time, as it's an accepting it 'cause you don't do anything else, which is a real sort of schizophrenic place to be.

TCB: *[Laughs and nods]* The book.

AGH: Yeah. *[Laughter]* It really is. And I think because of what we deal with it is not easy. The way you deal with it is not easy for people to read. Nobody, I think, would say that *The Salt Eaters* isn't a meaningful book to read. *[Laughter]*

Even though there are people who sort of took to it like the proverbial duck to the water, you pick it up and you say, "Hahhh, ahhh, I know." There's that sort of instant recognition and you just read it and you just love it. But I think the experience of most people is that they have to work at it. I know that one of the reasons why I wrote that article that I did write on *The Salt Eaters* is because I knew that book was so important, that everybody needs to read it. Writing an article on it doesn't begin to, you know, say everything and make it clear, but at least if it helps do that, that's something. So, I'm just sort of wondering how difficult will this one be? [Referring to the new novel] And then to the whole question of difficulty, is it the same? You start to wonder what is making it so difficult. The little sort of things—is it too hard for you [readers] to deal with because it's too hard to deal with? Or, are you sort of trying not to on some level? But I'm just wondering will that also be a hard book in that sense?

TCB: I have no idea because, I mean, that ain't my job. I am writing a book. *[Laughter]*

AGH: True. That's true.

TCB: Also, those are never the questions on my mind. No, no, that's never on my mind. It'd be on my mind if I was teaching the book.

AGH: Yeah.

TCB: It would be if I were for the first time in my life teaching it. I mean, it's weird. It's a weird book to teach. *[Laughter]* But *Blessing* is a much more linear kind of book. Each chapter is a particular day in the life of this family and this community, and this neighborhood. There's nothing tricky going on, you know?

AGH: Okay. *[Laughter]*

TCB: And the book, itself, is wrapped around by a prologue and an epilogue, which starts off you are on the porch with a broom wondering where your kid is. And at the end, you know, you were watching Iran Contragate wondering, you know, what kind of deal Congress has made. You had mentioned several connections to what's going on domestically.

AGH: Right.
TCB: Right. So, it's a straight book.

AGH: Okay. *[Laughter from crowd and Hull]*
TCB: Your basic eighth-grade reader. I'd say what it looks at must be hard because it certainly was hard to write. It broke my hope. It's hard to write because it's hard to look at. I think the Atlanta situation was hard to look at in many ways, the same as the Philadelphia situation. You don't know what to do with that. (People you know well; I'm thinking not so much of Mayor Wilson Goode. I'm thinking particularly of Maynard Jackson, the mayor of Atlanta, who is beloved.) I mean, Maynard is hip, he is wonderful, and there are any number of wonderful people who've just betrayed us and who couldn't pump up their hearts, had no faith in the people.

But, on the other hand, they'll protect the community by not opening up the story, which is exactly what we always thought it was—the Klan, ultra-right terrorists groups, the death squadrons, mercenaries practicing over here before they go over there. It's hard because that's your friend that fell by the wayside and then lied to you. That makes this hard to write and it's certainly hard to live. I mean, I don't know anybody in Atlanta in those years, who, especially in that community, wasn't stark raving mad, having gone through that treachery. I don't know anybody in that city who wasn't crazy and didn't know that they were.

AGH: Right.
TCB: There were many of us who were. For example, in '81, my daughter and I went down to Sengora to visit Gloria Joseph and we thought we were cool. We were not in the center of things [murders in Atlanta]; we were not on the death route, we were not on the killer route—we had not been experiencing any of the things the mental hygienist kept telling us about over and over every night: bed wetting, withdrawal, denial—whole generation damaged. Night after night, we're being bombarded with these messages by the professional healer industry. And my daughter and I got down there and we did not let go of each other's hand. We noticed that people were reacting to us strongly. We thought we were cool. We were crazy—we were stark raving mad. We could not sleep; we could not let go of each other. I could not allow

her out of my sight and that was in February of '81. I remember my daughter, for example, helping Gloria Joseph tie up the tomato vines with the stake with little rags and it was the first time she had let go of my hand.

AGH: Oh.

TCB: We slept together—my daughter is big. *[Laughter]* We're not talking about a little child. We're talking about serious sharing of the bed. *[Laughter]* And years later she allowed me to keep that nightmare alive in the house long enough to get this damn book finished before all my feelings came out . . .

AGH: Right.

TCB: In 1987, I'm typing a letter to Gloria saying, hello or whatever—whatever year it was. And she was up to her hip in plaster after having fallen in the pool, which is kind of a wonderful thing, you know? *[Laughter]* And I yelled up to my daughter and said, "Karma, do you have any little thing you wanna say to Aunt Doc Locks?"; that's what we call her, Doc Locks.

AGH: Okay. *[Laughter]*

TCB: And I wanna make this letter long because she's in bed and, you know, may need something to read; this is like a visit. *[Laughter]* And my daughter said, "Well, what's the matter?" And I said, "Well, she broke her hip cleaning out the pool." And Karma said, "Well, tell her I said, 'Doc Locks, anytime the pool needed to be cleaned out, I'll come and clean it out' and then that will free her up to work in the garden and to strangle the tomatoes." *[Laughter]* And that image, "strangle the tomatoes," my God, it goes all the way back to 1981 when you could not pick up any rope and tie vines without that Atlanta thing in your head, you know? And, yeah, it's hard.

AGH: Yeah.

TCB: *[Bambara starts to cry a bit but composes herself]* Yeah, it's hard. It's hard for me.

AGH: *[At this point Hull turns to audience for participation]* Is there anybody here that wants to ask about that?

Audience Question: *[Audience member asks Bambara how she felt about writing a novel as opposed to a documentary. Wants to know if she felt the novel allowed her to explore things the documentary could not].*

TCB: Yeah. In 1979, 1980, 1981, 1982, no one, repeat, no one could trust the kind of fact—information that was made available. No one. Not even the investigators. Everybody knew that there was a misinformation campaign going on. Everybody knew that there had been evidence destroyed. Everyone knew that there were secret informants running back and forth; that the FBI was conducting two investigations of their own, which they kept privately to themselves—one was black, one was white. Everybody knew that the Georgia Bureau of Investigation was doing two independent investigations; one on top, one on the bottom. Everybody knew. Within the APD you had two police departments, one black, one white. So, it was like mad—it was madness. Nobody had the facts, not even the killers. And by that, I mean, the particular mercenary squadrons, survivalists as they're called. And, you know, Klan thugs and a group of medical folks, renegade creeps from this . . . are we on tape? That gets me—no, that's a serious question 'cause it gives me another question as to why it's a novel: because of libel. So, now that I said that on tape, I need to be cool. *[Laughter]* You know, it is a real question. Security is a real question.

AGH: I know.

TCB: Because people do not come to your aid when you ask for security. They will say, "Well, she's weird." She had some problems, you know? So later for you, I ain't gonna answer no more questions. *[She laughs to let Hull know she is joking.]*

But one of the reasons that it is a novel is because I am a novelist. I am not an investigative journalist. Another reason is that you can get at the truth if you're not stumbling over well-placed, truly placed facts, missed facts, or unfacts. The other thing too, as they say, there was nothing trustworthy about any of the information that was available. I went to the professional investigators, the community-based investigators. All I had is the imagination and fifty years of having lived in this country, which is a lot.

That's what helped me. And that's why I say it's really peculiar that now so much evidence has been unearthed that the novel reads like a god damn documentary. Which makes me a little crazy. It's just clearly crazy. It's really crazy.

AGH: Oh, it is crazy. You know, the other thing I was thinking when you were reading that excerpt is Mama Lovey's position there in the middle of that confrontation with her grandson. It almost reminded me of the position of Velma and Minnie in *Salt Eaters* who are really, literally in every way, at the center of the novel. Of course I noticed that the people who are at the center of the novel, are these two women. Velma heals, then you know. At the same time her healing takes place you know the central role that Velma played in the community and all of that. How are women centered, if they are, in this book?

TCB: I don't know.

AGH: Okay.

TCB: No. *[Laughs and smiles to reveal that she is joking with Hull again.]* One of the reasons I don't know; what I mean is I have not looked at the manuscript lately. I'm trying to, you know, get it out of my head so I can come at it differently to edit it relentlessly. *[Laughter]* But there are a number of groups of women in the book that I can call up. One is a group of women workers. I don't know to what degree this actually happened during the Atlanta period, but it happened often enough that, I guess, I could make a case that under the guise of concern for the children, the idea that women belonged in the home was revived. You know, women workers were having a tough time in the offices and in the plants in Atlanta.

AGH: Sort of "What are you doing out here?" *[Crosstalk]*

TCB: Right, because these kids are being murdered because they're being neglected on account of women are working. So get on out of here . . .

AGH: Right.

TCB: Children don't have anybody at home, so women working had to fight that battle all over again. I can recall in Atlanta at Stover and Steel. And there's some big issue about absenteeism among women workers and I said, "Well, you know, until such time as nurturing is 50/50, that women who have children sick (it's just left up to the women, that mother is who stays home). So, either we give women workers more absentee time or we establish a 50/50 nurturing at this plant. The boss cannot establish that, then we need more time for women workers." Then the boss jumped up in my face, "Oh, don't come in here starting that stuff. I'll have you know, I run an equal opportunity household . . ." *[Audience laughter]* There are any number of situations in the book, it's sort of minor, that is to say, you catch them as we go through: Characters riding the bus, women workers talking, you know, in the middle of the day, coming away from the plant caucus on the bus because it's one of the few places that you could talk 'cause the laundry rooms were no longer women's territory because that's where children go. That's women territory, it's where children go and people are really concerned now about closing all of those areas down where children are—skating rinks, playgrounds, etc. So, that meant women workers are kinda talking to each other on the bus about what's going on in the offices and in the plant. Anyway, that's one of the groups of women that pop up every now and then. That's a voice that we hear a lot—the women workers in Atlanta.

Audience Question: *[Inaudible comment]*
TCB: I hope the question was when is the book out? I hope in the fall of '88 it will be out. *[Laughter]* It'll be a Random Vintage book, paperback so it won't cost thirty dollars and stuff.

AGH: Yeah, just fifteen.
TCB: Yeah. *[Laughter from audience]*

Audience Question: *[Asks her to discuss the themes in her films and scripts]*
TCB: I moved into TV documentary a couple of years ago, primarily because I wanted to become a filmmaker. But I didn't want to practice on my money, you know? *[Laughter from audience]*

Also, I wanted to do documentary—having finished the Atlanta book, I would say, I don't know what the word is, hmmm hmmm hmmm, appreciative of how much I needed a documentary discipline to curtail that fictional speed. So I thought, "documentaries are cool." Also the fact that I happened to run into a TV documentary producer/director [Louis Massiah] and we hit it off, you know, very well. Love at first sight.

So, we did two films together. We did two documentaries together—one *The Bombing of Osage Avenue*, which I showed the other night here at the Women's Employment and Resource Corporation, founded by my cousin Carol Lewis, which is about the so-called MOVE incident in Philadelphia, city of brotherly love on the day after Mother's Day in 1985. The film has been around a lot. It has moved about quite a bit and it's won a slew of very prestigious awards. It has broken through a silence, most especially in Philadelphia. I mean, people don't understand why Ramona Africa is still in jail? Or, is Louis James gonna get her house, and is somebody gonna stand trial? What about the guy who said he would take full responsibility? Is he gonna stand trial? It began to break through a silence; a tremendously imposed silence. Not only in Philadelphia about that case, but a lot of other places about similar situations.

And then I did a film about Cecil Moore who may or may not be known in this part of the world. Moore was an attorney during the sixties in North Philadelphia. One of the wonderful things about Cecil was he never operated out of self-interest, which is really funny to me. For example, he was a liquor salesman and he spearheaded the movement against the tap rooms that were destroying the neighborhoods in North Philadelphia. He was a marine, but he was constantly pulling the covers off the armed services. He was constantly demystifying all that patriotic crap. He was a lawyer but he was continually giving people—judges—a hard time and calling them on the bench. He was clean, constantly clean, but hung out on the block. He was not interested in fancy places; just a very beautiful man. Kind of an Adam Clayton Powell type. In fact, they were good friends; brash, style, cigars. He had a very similar style. So it was a real pleasure to do a piece on Cecil.

Except that one of the difficulties of working on that—it really kind of drove me crazy—is I had originally structured it as a social action primer. I wanted to know what makes people be involved? How do people change? What makes people risk? But everyone we talked to who called themselves Cecil's people (at one time when Cecil took over NAACP they said it's not the National Association for the Advancement of Colored People; it is National Association for the Advancement of Cecil's) *[Laughter]* talk about Cecil they make a legendary, epic, God reification thing. Which strikes me as very dangerous because once you begin to remove a leader from the realm of the realistic, you remove them also from the realm of the replicable. And it's like if we cannot duplicate those lessons then what is the point? It's like cutting a man's feet off. As though he did not exist in our community and we did not nurture that. But at any rate, those are some of the pieces I began doing when I got to Philadelphia, which helped me learn, tremendously, Philadelphia. Now I feel competent and bold and arrogant to do what I want to do, which are feature films.

The one I am doing now is the take over of a luxury building by the homeless. It started as a short story. I went to the homeless union of Philadelphia and said, "What do you think of this story?" So, in October the International Homeless Union stopped off at Philadelphia. They took over a couple of buildings. Yeah, I want to do feature films.

AGH: If you start concentrating on feature films does that mean you will do less writing? Or does that feed back into the writing in some way that nurtures it, changes it?

TCB: I don't know. I don't know. It's all the work. Organizing is the work and writing is the work, and raising children is the work.

AGH: It sounds like as long as you are doing the work and it is going into some type of package, it doesn't matter that it is this or that or that or whatever else if they all feel equally right at the time that you are doing them? It is not that you have to get the work out in writing. It's not that this particular piece of the work has to be packaged in a film?

TCB: Yes. But let me put it this way: I cannot imagine that I would be interested in doing a film on *The Salt Eaters*.

AGH: Even though there's a lot of cinematic stuff in there?

TCB: Even now or then.

AGH: It would not have been a film?

TCB: No. I would not want to do the homeless take over as a short story. I very much want to do it as a film. I cannot adapt short stories for a film— maybe for puppet shows, but not for a film.

AGH: I just want to ask you about the whole aspect of spirituality that is so important a part of contemporary black women's writing. It is one of the things that people have to get comfortable, at least familiar, with to find their way through *The Salt Eaters*. I am concerned with how we don't yet have the means, the vocabulary, and the wherewithal to talk about that in the way that it really manifests in people's work. For example, when people talk about Toni Morrison and bring up the term *magic realism* that is not quite getting to it. I spent two years in Jamaica and I was very aware that the same kind of spirituality shows up in literature there. . . . It is an aspect of all the women's writing of the diaspora.

So you begin to see how really important it is. It is also about these modalities that we term new age types of things. But we have not quite pinned that down yet. But I guess what I want to ask you is in our work and beyond what do you make of that kind of emphasis? And I guess I could also talk about works like Paule Marshall's *Praise Song for the Widow*. What do you make of that phenomenon?

TCB: It is not surprising to find it there. I don't know how to talk about it usefully.

AGH: But I feel like we need something to talk about it.

TCB: I know I don't know how to talk usefully about that spiritual dimension in the writing. But the one kind of book that makes at least one aspect of it available are the books that are based in ritual healing. I am thinking *[inaudible]* and Leslie Marmon Silko's *Ceremony*, and *The Salt Eaters*.

Books where the very shape of the book itself is a ceremony, a series of steps, a process that the author is taking the protagonist through but also asking the reader to go through. In other words, I am inclined to say it's not only that the atmosphere of the book is informed by a spiritual culture but also that you are put through some kind of process with that. And the process that is most immediately recognizable seems to be a human ritual. The other I can't get at. I know what you mean. I can't get at it. I am not surprised but I'm glad to see it.

AGH: I'm glad too but it looks like it's something we can talk about if we figure out how to do that.

Audience Question: *[Person asks about the spiritual dimension in Bambara's new book and the interaction between the characters Sundiata and Mama Lovey.]*
TCB: There is this wonderful film by Julie Dash where the camera is panning the graveyard in the Sea Islands. And you know in the Sea Islands when you bury your Uncle Thomas who is an electrician, you have to take some fuses and stick them in the grave among the clam shells as part of the decoration. And then there is the moss hanging down from oak trees and there is this moment of magic, a little riff that is looped, and then the ancestors come out of the trees for a moment. I keep looking at the directions to indicate that this is another dimension or whatever. So then music speeds or slows down or something and the movie moves on. To do that in film is fairly simple. That is to say there is a cinematic vocabulary, where talking about or demonstrating dimensions on the page is not so easy unless you have an eight-track deck mouth. *[Audience laughter]* In print it is not so easy. I'm trying because we pretend not to know. Yeah, I'm still looking for ways.

AGH: One last thing I want to say is I can't wait to get my hands on *Till Blessings Come.*[1] Every time I read *The Salt Eaters* different things happen. *[She reads from a passage in the book about gathering in the woods]* ". . . gatherings demand, stay with you, lock you into particular sight. The eyes will not let you let it go." I think reading rich work like this is like that. It reminded me of something people are saying now because we are talking about deconstructive theory. They say that every reading is a misreading in the sense that you see what you see but that entails leaving out all the rest of the things you could see. For instance, the first time that I read *Salt Eaters* and wrote about it I was locked into looking at what it was I wrote about. And when I looked at it again I saw a little bit more of that; I saw some of the same kind of thing. But the last time I looked at it the one thing I was focused on was language.

I would like to talk about how everyone in the book is defined by language. Now, doing that brings up for me how many African American critics at this point focus on language. And a lot of this emphasis does come from looking at poststructuralist and deconstructive theory. There is a lot that we can be ambivalent about for that. What it raised for me is something else that you said: "Why do you need that way of talking about it if we have already talked about it?" You had a phrase there [referring to theory and *The Salt Eaters*] that struck me. You mentioned [critics] being anesthetized by dazzling performances with somebody else's aesthetic. Which in a sense you could see it that way, but just that whole focus there on language becomes something interesting. What do you see and how do you talk about it? It pulls a lot of things together and it also keeps us on guard about how we are going to do it. Do we need Derrida to give us permission to talk about these things in these ways? Do you have any sort of reactions to that?

TCB: No. *[Laughter from Hull and the audience]* Except it's always occurred to me reading, I think it is very characteristic of African American writers. . . . I was just pausing to think if it's also true of other communities of other aesthetics, the . . . how do you put it . . . critical theory? No, critical base . . . no . . . at any rate, it's in the book [meaning African American texts]. It's always in the book. I mean, Langston Hughes informs you how to talk about Langston Hughes *[nods her head]*.

Audience Question: *[Not very clear but something about Americans being in a state of amnesia and what people can do. Suggests using film to disseminate information.]*

TCB: Well, it would be noble sounding if I said yes. I'm interested in film for the filmmaker. That's the impulse, the drive—it has always been—to make films. Writing to me has always meant an apprenticeship. I mean, I would write whether there is a publishing industry or not because it keeps me from being crazy. But I'm a filmmaker. I have always been a filmmaker—to me.

AGH: Well, hey, it has been nice talking to you. Thank you. *[Bambara nods agreement]*

---

1. She means *If Blessing Comes*, which is eventually published as *Those Bones Are Not My Child*.

How She Came by Her Name

Louis Massiah/1994

From *Deep Sightings and Rescue Missions: Fiction, Essays, & Conversations* by Toni Cade Bambara, edited by Toni Morrison (Pantheon, 1996). Reprinted by permission of Hatch-Billops Collection, Inc.

Louis Massiah: I would like to start by asking Toni Cade Bambara how she came by her name.

Toni Cade Bambara: I earned it, and I worked hard for it. I've had several names. When I was an undeclared music major in college, my name was Tonal Cadence, or occasionally Tonal Cadenza or Tonal Coda. When I was in the psychiatric community, my given name, Miltona, was changed to Miltown. At my fiftieth birthday celebration in Atlanta I was given a new name and in a very serious manner. My feet were bathed, my head was anointed with oil, and a group of young women called Sisters in Blackness gave me the name Hanifa. For the last five years I have been trying to get comfortable with that name, but whenever I look at the name there are two scenarios that unfold, neither one of which I can get with. One is Hanifa on horseback dressed as a man during the Crusades, brandishing a sword and shouting, "Death to the Infidels!" In my postmenopausal journey toward wise womanishness, this is a little bit too martial for me. The other Hanifa is Hanifa the Hidden, moving from safe house to safe house, trying to get to the waterfront in order to sneak aboard a ship and get away from the mob of mullahs who are out in the street brandishing swords yelling, "Death to the Blasphemer!" since Hanifa the health worker has been speaking publicly on the rape of the young children who wind up in her clinic. For the most part I've been living my life out loud, so I don't think I need that lesson in particular. So, for five years I have been trying to get comfortable with the name Hanifa because I take it very seriously when a sector of the community that names me "daughter, mother, sister" takes the trouble to find some other name to call out some other aspect of me that they see.

I was born with the name Miltona Mirkin Cade. My mother informs me that my father, Walter Cade II, intended to have all his children named after him. My brother became Walter Cade III, but when it came to Walter Mae or Walterina, my mother put her foot down. So my father then named me after his employer in that great plantation tradition. Those of you of my generation who grew up in Harlem or who are older than I am can remember hundreds of people who came up on the Dixieland Express to work on Colonel Black's plantation, also known as Chock Full O' Nuts, and how those workers always named their first- or second-born after Colonel Black or his wife, Page. Every time I run across a Page, I ask, "Did your folks work for Chock Full O' Nuts?" Once a season Colonel Black would have his namesakes and their families up to his estate in Tarrytown, near the Rockefellers. There would be watermelon and fried chicken and stuff. He would sometimes hand out a savings bond to his namesakes. Milton Mirkin, the person I was named after, was not forthcoming with any savings bonds or any watermelons. I didn't even know the man, except I think I met him once. It is just a shred of a memory, which I will share.

Whenever I come through the garment center or when I see a really well-made Milano straw hat, I get this little memory. Or whenever I see the film *Klute.* Whenever I am in a place with clothing racks and tailoring tables, I get this memory. I am walking down the aisles between tables, and I am around four years old. I have on patent-leather Mary Janes and frilly socks. I have on my navy blue swing A-line coat with brass buttons, and this most wonderful red Milano straw hat with a satin sash tied at the side. I am trying to hold my daddy's hand, but he is using his hands to talk. There is a white man way at the end of this aisle of tables wearing big pants and standing astride like he's somebody. My father's voice is not familiar to me, and as we walk to the white man my father gets smaller and smaller. So I let go of his hand and step away from him. He turns to look at me and I pretend to loosen the sash on my hat. This is just a shred of a memory, but I bring it up by way of indicating what my relationship to that given name was. At some point, around kindergarten age, I accosted my mother, who was trying to take a bath. I was leaning against the hamper, and I announced to Mother that my name was Toni, and it was not short for Miltona, it was Toni, period. She was very indulgent and said, "Yes, sure, Honey." I guess like any other kid, I was always coming up with names. Whenever you get a new doll, you start coming up with names, and sometimes the names are too wonderful for your dolls, so you take them for yourself. I don't know where the name Toni came from, although in those days there was Toni home permanent. In second grade I did have a Toni doll, which had legs that didn't move, it didn't do anything, but you could comb the hell out of its hair, set it with sugar and water, and the staples would hold!

My friends and my family began calling me Toni, but at school it was still Miltona, which I tried not to answer to. I tried to make people call me Toni. Years later in the fourth grade, I am in Brooklyn and there is a singing star named Toni Harper who is singing a song called "The Candy Store Blues." Once again I struggled to make this name my own. In the fifth grade we moved to New Jersey; I got possession of my school record, and with ink eradicator and a nib-point pen I did some choice forgery, but I didn't do it completely, so there were still papers and cards with the name Miltona Mirkin Cade, so I was still struggling with the name. By the time I got to college, it was all over. It was Toni Cade.

The Bambara is in many ways more complicated to talk about, but I'll give the short version. It's 1970 and Mom and I are in Atlanta, which was where she grew up, and she is trying to find her mother's grave, and I am toting around an African art book. I am also "tumbling big." For the last few months I had been trying to find a name for this child. I hit on Bene as a middle name. Jane Karina and Barumba kept giving me these complicated Harero names that I couldn't spell or pronounce or remember without calling them up. Bene, which means "child of," became a middle name. Then Karma, which was her first name, was on everybody's lips: "This is your karma, this is my karma." So I said, "Karma!" Then there was the problem of the last name. I didn't know what "Cade" meant, but I always liked Cade. It was short, but not too blunt, kind of mysterious. It wasn't "Johnson." I felt very at home in the name Toni Cade. So I am looking around for a name, but I didn't want to change the name completely because I wanted people from kindergarten to remember me.

I have always been very fond of the Chiwaras. The Chiwaras are made by the Dogon and the Bambaras. I tried out Dogon first: Karma Bene Dogon. Well, that sounds like, "Karma Bene, well doggone!" That didn't work and Toni Cade Dogon definitely did not work! Then it became Bambara. Karma Bene Bambara. That worked. Toni Cade Bambara—the minute I said it I immediately inhabited it, felt very at home in the world. This was my name. It is not so unusual for an artist, a writer, to name themselves; they are forever constructing themselves, are forever inventing themselves. That's the nature of that spiritual practice. Maya Angelou changed her name. Toni Morrison definitely changed her name—Chloe Wofford?!! Audre Lorde changed the spelling of her first and last names. It's not all that peculiar. So that's where my name comes from.

LM: As a very young child growing up in New York City, you did something that most of our parents told us not to do. You talked to strangers.
TCB: Yes, and I went into their houses too.

LM: Could you talk about what gave you the freedom to talk to strangers, and who were some of those people you talked with?
TCB: We lived on 151st Street between Broadway and Amsterdam, which is a very long block, and there were thousands of families on that block. There were also thousands of families in my building. Many people kept their doors open, which I thought was wonderful because I was very nosy! There was a family up on the fifth floor, and I used to pass their door going to the roof. There were thousands of relatives in this apartment, and if you stepped in or even looked in they always said, "You want something to eat?" And I would say, "Yeah." They would feed me things I would never eat at home, like liver and onions on a biscuit made with water and lard! They were wonderful people except that they beat their children. They beat those children!

There were also some "ladies of the night." (That's what my mother used to call them.) They used to lend out their back room to black longshoremen who were attempting to organize against Murder Incorporated. I used to hang out and listen to them. There were lots of meetings and rallies going on in that period. I was born in 1939, and the radical thirties were still spilling over in the forties. There was still that notion that an active political life was a perfectly normal thing. People had to organize against the crackdown forces which, in those days, was the police, the FBI, Immigration, the Draft Board, and the Mob, which are pretty much the crackdown forces today, except people don't acknowledge Mob participation too much.

I went to P.S. 186 on 145th and Broadway, and I would walk to school along Broadway. As people were cranking out the awning in the morning, I would say "Hi" and stop and talk. Of course, I would be late to school, always. When I came out of school, I would come around the Amsterdam Avenue way, which was very exciting. There was the Brown Bomber Bar and Grill. There was Walker's Barbecue. There were hand laundries that used to keep J. A. Rogers pamphlets in the window and would sometimes stick them in your laundry and charge you for them. There were wonderful barbershops, and the men would come out and do all that male choreography; hoisting their pants and the like. They would have hats, and gold teeth, and they would talk. I would always stop and eavesdrop. Sometimes they would recognize me as the kid who turns in at 151st Street where the brewery is. Sometimes they would send me on errands. They'd say, "Hey, you little honey, when you turn in, you know that house next to the brewery? Walk up the stoop, knock on the right-hand window, and tell the lady we are going to bring the petition around." So I became this little messenger. Also on that block was this wonderful beauty parlor where *everything* got discussed. I mean *everything*! So I definitely used to lean against the window, and sometimes I would slide in and sit down and listen to stuff. That beauty parlor is not there anymore. A Dairy Queen is there now, with the most wonderful sign that says:

> THERE WILL BE NO LOITERING.
> THERE WILL BE NO PROFANE LANGUAGE.
> THERE WILL BE NO CREDIT.
> CURTESY OF THE MANGLEMENT.

I talked to people who seemed interested in me. Because we came from a tiny family (my mother was an orphan, and my father was the son of a runaway), I was always looking for grandmothers, because I didn't have any, and everybody else had some. People had grandmothers with them plus grandmothers down South to go to. This seemed extravagant to me; I wanted some. I wanted uncles and cousins, which I didn't have, so I began adopting people in the same way people adopted me. I had relatives, so to speak, that had never met my mother. They were just people in the neighborhood who thought I was interesting, who wanted to talk to me, or who recognized that I was available.

To answer your question as to what made me able to do that, I have no idea. Loneliness impelled me; curiosity keeps me doing it.

LM: You dedicate *The Salt Eaters* to your mother for giving you the literal space to create. Could you talk about your mother as an influence in your artistic development?

TCB: My mother had put herself through school wanting to be a journalist with the *New York Age*, but instead got married and went into civil service. I always think of her as a shadow artist in the sense that that is her take on things. I have been trying to encourage her to be a mystery writer because she really has that kind of suspicious mindset! My mother was not a house-proud woman, but she had a thing about these bookcases that she bought in Macy's basement, unfinished furniture division, and every spring she would spread the paper, get a rag, take the books out, dust them, and then she would repaint these bookcases a sparkling white. I would look at these books, and one of the books was a little, skinny, flat, black book with a little bronze insert, *Bronzeville*, by Miss Gwendolyn Brooks. It had pictures of children, so I kind of thought it was mine. I used to read it and take it to my room, but it wasn't my book, so I would bring it back and put it in the bookcase. I would hear the name Gwen Brooks because I lived in Harlem, and Harlem was a very rich, wealthy society in the sense that we had everybody. The Robesons had moved back in 1936. Camilla Williams was vocalizing up in the Harlem Y. Everybody in the world went to the Countee Cullen Branch, and to the Arthur Schomburg Collection (which is where I met John Henry Clarke). I would look at a poster of Gwen Brooks, and I liked her face. I like her name, Gwendolyn Brooks. It sounded very ordinary, and it sounded like it was possible to be a writer and to be ordinary.

Also in Mom's bookcase was Langston Hughes's *The Big Sea*. The jacket had come off, leaving only the yellow book, so I didn't see his picture, and I didn't know for years that Langston Hughes was the Mr. Langdon who used to come into the library and talk to us. When I was in the fifth grade, I was going to school in the Bronx, but we lived on Morningside Avenue, and though the Mount Morris library was not the closest branch, it was the most interesting because those ladies really knew books; and they were interested in making you read. If you were taking out two books, they would recommend a third. Langston Hughes lived diagonally across the street, and he would break three rules that endeared him to me forever. First of all, he would come into the library and would not take off his hat. Not because he was rude, but because he was loaded down with a briefcase, portfolio, a satchel of books: he was coming to work. He had great hats. He had a Borsalino that I would really like to have. The second violation was he would come into the children's section. As you know, in those days age borders were very strict and they were heavily patrolled. If you were little, then you went over here, and you listened to Sunday school stories; if you were a grown-up, you were over there listening to the senior choir. If you were in the movies, you were in the children's section, roped off with that lady in the white dress with the flashlight to hit you with and keep you all in check. The rest of the movie house was for the grown-ups.

It was the same thing with the library. So, Mr. Langdon (as we thought he was called) would come into the children's library, would stroll along the windowsill; looking at the sweet potato plants stuck with toothpicks hanging in the wide-mouth amber jars, and he would comment on them. We would always be looking at him thinking, Is he the stranger our parents always warned us against? Was he the pervert we had to watch out for? What was he doing in the children's library? Then he would come and sit down with us and spread out his work. He was always very careful about space. If his book hit yours, he would say "Excuse me." I can't tell you how rare that was in those days. Nobody had respect for children or their sense of space. Well, he would be writing, reading, and pondering, and then he would look up and break the third rule—he would talk. He would ask us what we're doing. What kind of homework we have. Do we think it is intelligent homework? What was on our minds? The man was a knockout!

So, why I dedicated *The Salt Eaters* to my mom: I can remember any number of times my mother, unlike other parents, would walk around us if we were daydreaming. If she was mopping, she would mop around us. My mother had great respect for the life of the mind. Between working her two jobs, she would put one foot in her stocking and would go into this deep stare. She too had the need for daydreaming and for talking with herself. She didn't get much of an occasion with a mouthy kid like me.

I was writing stories long before I learned to spell. My father used to get the *Daily Mirror* (which my mother thought was an antilabor paper), and there were very fat margins, so I would scribble in the margins. When I had someone captive, like my mother in the bathtub, I would read this scribble-scrabble to her and she would listen. Essentially, it was my mother's respect for the life of the mind. She gave us permission to be artists. After my first aptitude test I was made aware that I was a freak in some way. In those aptitude tests they would say. "If you have a half hour to spare, would you build a wagon, take apart a clock and see how it works?" etc. They never said, "Daydream, just sit in a window and stare. Conjure up characters and plot stories." They never said that. My mother made it all very casual. My brother was something of a prodigy in terms of art and music, and so her thing was to give us access. To give us access to materials, to museums, to libraries, to parks. We figured that one of her motivations was that she had been kind of shy about going to these places, but she became emboldened as a mother. We always had equipment. We had no furniture or much in the way of wardrobes, but we had drawing paper, paints, and raffia to make mats. We had books and a piano. In the fourth grade I went to the Modern School run by Miss Mildred Johnson, sister of James "Dark Manhattan" Johnson.

She was very mean, very yellow, very strict, and very snooty. She would look down at me coming in there with hand-me-down clothes. I didn't come in a cab like most of the other students. The other kids would talk about going up to Martha's Vineyard for the weekend, or going to Sugarbush to ski. They went to Europe and to the Met. They were black people, but they were not my people. It was confusing. We would take our early lessons in French, and in the afternoon we were learning about the medieval guilds of Europe. I was totally out of it. But Miss Francis, my teacher, wrote a report home and said, "She's making a very difficult social adjustment, but she evidences talent in creative writing."

LM: Where did you learn your first political lessons? Who were you listening to?

TCB: The radical thirties were not over with in the early forties, so there were people running around the neighborhood setting up meetings and rallies. And I lived in Harlem with black bookstores, such as Micheaux's Liberation Memorial Bookstore—"the home of proper propaganda"—and with Speakers' Corner. I do not think a community is viable without a Speakers' Corner. If we can't hear black people speak, we become captive to the media, and we disacknowledge Blackspeak. Our ears are no longer attuned to any kind of sensible talk. I knew that Speakers' Corner was valuable, because when we left Harlem most people seemed to be kind of airheads. They were not raising critical questions. There was no street culture. They were stupid compared to Harlemites, who were sharp and cynical. My kind of folks. Everybody spoke at Speakers' Corner, from center to left. You didn't have too many right-wing jerks getting up on that soapbox. Who would speak were people like the women from the Sanctified Church, and they might talk about the research they were doing on the Colored People's Conventions of the Reconstruction era. Trade unionists, definitely, talking about the need for a black coalition, which we have now—the Coalition of Black Trade Unionists. The members of the Harlem branch of the Communist party might give an analysis of candidates running on the ward level, city level, or national level. Members of the various Socialist parties would get up and talk about the state, the circumstances, conditions, and status of workers throughout the world and why there needed to be solidarity, etc. The Abyssinians (now called Rastas) would get up and talk about African civilizations and why we needed to support Haile Selassie. Temple people (now called Muslims) would talk about how they were catching hell back in Chicago and Detroit from the government. Why stateside black folks needed to be in solidarity with West Indians and East Indians coming into the community. West Indians would get up and speak. Folks would talk about how the Puerto Ricans were coming into the neighborhood, and we ought not be xenophobic. The U.S. government was bringing truckloads of Puerto Ricans into Harlem in 1948, which was around the time of the Nationalist party formation, which is why they were bringing in people from Puerto Rico to break that independence movement up. Speakers on the corner would explain all that. Then the Puerto Ricans would get up and speak, and people would try not to laugh at the accents.

So Speakers' Corner made it easy to raise critical questions, to be concerned about what's happening locally and internationally. It shaped the political perceptions of at least three generations. It certainly shaped mine, and I miss it today. There is no Speakers' Corner where I live. There is no outdoor forum where people can not only learn the word, hear information, hear perspective, but also learn how to present information, which is also what I learned on Speakers' Corner: how to speak and leave spaces to let people in so that you get a call-and-response. You also learn how to speak outdoors, which is no small feat. You also have to learn how to not be on paper, to not have anything between you and the community that names you. So I learned a great many things, and I am still grounded in orality, in call-and-response devices, and I do not deliver papers. I am frequently asked to give a paper at a conference and I refuse. I say that I don't do papers unless I am being paid to write an essay that is going to be published somewhere that I know of. But I am not doing a talk and a paper. People then ask me to give a talk. Well, I can do that. I prepare as hard as anybody else in order to be able to make eye contact with people I am talking to. One of the reasons I do that is I am very shy and I don't like being shy, so I make a point of wrestling with that, and one way is to constantly remove any kind of camouflage or any kind of barrier that exists between me and the community that names me.

My mother gave us the race thing. She also encouraged us in an interventionist style. At school we were not to sing "Old Black Joe." We were not to take any shit, and we were to report back to her any stereotypic or racist remark. This was difficult because shit was happening all the time. For example, I had a really fascist teacher in the third grade, Miss Beaks. She did all sorts of things that were really out. I wrote a story once called "The Making of a Snitch." It was published when I was in high school, and it's about the period of the late forties when, as Gerald Home would say, "the National policy shifted from blacks as inferior to blacks as subversive." We were constantly getting pressure in that McCarthy period. When anything weird went on in school, the teacher would grab one person at a time and take him or her into the cloakroom and encourage and bribe the person to rat on classmates. I wrote that story, and many years later I rewrote it when I ran into the classmate who had been made into a snitch in those early days and then turned up in the late fifties as a government agent. He was working the crowd in front of the Hotel Theresa when Malcolm (who was like our mayor) was there, certainly the appropriate person to welcome Fidel to Harlem.

In those days teachers set traps for you. There was this kid Michael who sat three rows over. We used to walk home together because he lived one block from me. He was a very quiet kid, very repressed. The teacher would always lure him into saying something so that she would be able to call his mother to school. His mother would come and strap him with a Sam Browne belt. Most parents would come and beat their children in front of the class. When I would hear at meetings or at Speakers' Corner about the brutality of slavery, I began to connect this as behavior learned and carried over, and I would hope that there would one day be a rehab camp. I still think that. What do we do with snitches like Earl Anthony, who had been a friend of mine, and now reveals himself in a new book as having been a government agent all those years when he was with the Panther party? What do we do with people like that? If you believe in transformation politics, or transformation psychology, you feel that they can change. But we don't have rehabilitation centers to send them to. When I was in Laos in the summer of 1975, in Vientiane City, at the last moment of liberation they sent the generals to the Plain of Jars, which had been carpet-bombed, to share the hardships of the peasants, to live with them and to turn the Plain of Jars into a green haven. The generals went to school six hours a week, learning Marxist-Leninist doctrine, and they shared the hardships of the peasants. I found those kinds of camps in Vietnam, in North Korea, in China, and in Cuba. It's dodgy to set up a system like that because it can get, in a split second, totalitarian and inhumane, but we very much need something because we have so many walking wounded and defectives, not only agent types, but also people who are still stumbling around from the sixties who never were embraced quite enough, who got assigned things to do and then got left hanging, and are still walking blasted.

LM: When did you first realize the possibility of your writing, and when did you begin to think of yourself as a writer?

TCB: I never thought of myself as a writer. I always thought of myself as a community person who writes and does a few other things. I always get a little antsy when people limit me as a writer. In terms of scribbling, I've always been writing, so long as I could find paper—not easy during the war. My mother always had gorgeous legs, and my father had a very proprietary pride about her legs, so no matter how bad the market was, or how bad the budget was, she always had black silk stockings. These stockings came wrapped around a rectangle of paper. I couldn't wait for my mama to get her gorgeous legs into another pair of stockings so I could get that paper. I became something of a community scribe. People would say, "Hey, you little honey, run down to Miss Dorothy's house and help her write the letter to her nephew in the Navy." "Run up the way and tell them what happened at the meeting." "Hey, write this down." When I lived in Atlanta, I was a community scribe in the sense that people would hail me, "Excuse me, you the writin' lady?" "Yeah." "Pull in here into the gas station. The man wants to sell his Ford to this guy here. Can you write a contract?" "Sure." "Here's a paper bag and a pencil. Get to it." In return they would give me my inspection ticket stamped. People in the neighborhood would knock on my door. "You the writin' lady? Listen, the telephone company has screwed me again. Can you write a nasty letter?" Then they would pay me with Jell-O with fruit in it. Sometimes they would wrap up a dollar, which had been folded and folded and tied in a corner of a handkerchief. Take you a year to unwrap that dollar. So, I got paid as a community scribe and got trained as a community scribe very early.

When I came back from Cuba in 1973, I began to think that writing could be a way to engage in struggle, it could be a weapon, a real instrument for transformation politics. Let me take myself a little more seriously and stop just having fun, I thought.

Let me talk about my mother as "hero." There is a scene of a woman turning a school out in the title story "Gorilla, My Love," and I once did an article for *Redbook* on Mother's Day which was about my mother at school. In 1946, the United Nations was established in New York and everyone was very proud. They would drive us crazy in school with these assembly programs about the goddamn United Nations. We would have to draw posters for various campaigns about the United Nations. Very generic and very dull. Children holding hands around the globe. So we're drawing one day, and the teacher falls asleep. I am drawing the children around the globe, but now I want to give them color because my children are Chinese, Indian, and African. You know those school crayons, big and fat, but no matter how hard you pressed you could never get any color out of them. I did not want my children looking streaky and mud-colored. I wanted them to look cool. So I thought that if I got the coffee grinds out of Miss Beak's coffee cup, I could maybe get the right color. So I went up to her desk and woke her up to ask if I could have the coffee. She woke up like a bear. The first thing she said was, "What are you doing out of your seat? You take yourself too seriously in general and in particular." Well, I could handle that. But then she started really blowing like a hurricane, talking about "as ugly and crummy and lousy as these crayons are, they are good enough for you people because who the hell do you think you are? You are just poor colored children." Well, this was too big for me. This was a case for Mother. My mother had a turning-the-school outfit. She had a serious Joan Crawford hat and a Persian lamb coat. She wore one of two favorite suits—either an aquamarine suit with a cherub cameo, which I didn't like, or my favorite suit, a dark wine, red, wide-wale corduroy, and, of course, her gorgeous legs in the silk stockings. And some I. Miller outlet opera pumps. She was bad! Now, she would stride into the class and lay out the first law: "My children are never wrong, so you cannot be right." All the children would be so delighted because here was a woman come to champion her child, not humiliate, beat, torture, and terrorize everybody and make everybody throw up. The teacher would say, "Can we talk outside?" My mother was not moving. She also had this scary pocketbook. The click on it was like the cocking of a shotgun. Mom allowed how she was a substitute teacher, and she had pull with the Board of Education, she knew everybody, so "your ass is mine." She would start working her thing. She would be working the dimple in her chin, arching one eyebrow and getting this flinty edge to her very articulate voice, and the teacher would be coming apart. The second law: "You apologize to my daughter and you apologize to the class." The teacher would look at me and finally get my name right (the name my daddy gave me). Then she would turn to the class and try to present some lame story about how the coffee gave her nightmares and she ran amuck and lost her mind. My mother would be saying, "Apologize now or I'll meet you down at 110 Livingston Street." We would laugh at the teacher. Michael would not laugh. He never laughed at any so-called authority figure. He knew what would happen, but we all laughed at her. Then my mother swiveled on her I. Miller black suede opera pumps and moved out of the classroom with the sleeves of her Persian lamb moving like regal robes. Mother was therapeutic.

LM: When do you find your tribe?

TCB: Well, I felt very at home in Harlem as a child. I spent the first ten years of my life in Harlem. I had skates and got around a lot and met a lot of wonderful people. I met this one woman who had a tremendous influence on my writing. Dorothy McNorton lived across the street from us when we lived on Morningside. She taught me critical theory . . . another story for another day. In Mildred Johnson's school I did not feel at home, but it did teach me a lot about class. I think by the time I got to college I was hanging out in the Village. I began to identify my people as artist types, even though I was a biochem/premed major at the time, and those people were definitely not my people and that lifestyle was not mine. Like being up late at night in the stinky, smelly lab eating weird food out of a vending machine. I would try not to drop and break any test tubes because that was thirty-five cents, and we were on a really tight budget. I felt much more comfortable with art majors and hanging around the art department, so I used to model for art classes.

That lifestyle was more my thing. I liked the smell of linseed oil and turpentine, mainly because one of my spirit guides comes to me that way, namely my mother's mother; that is, her "visitations" are heralded by those odors—she painted. I also liked the theater group. Working so seriously on these dumb plays. I loved it! So I hung out with theater folk and art folk. But these were white people at Queens College, and they were not my people either. There were a couple of political types there, like Ellie Hakim, who started *Studies on the Left*, a journal still around today. This was the height of the McCarthy period, from 1955 to 1959. We had quite a collection of people at Queens. The granddaughter of Robert Ingersoll, the niece of Alexander Woollcott. But hanging out in the Village I got a little closer understanding of who my people were, as I was always looking for a job and I was underage. In the Village I would go over to Montmartre's Spaghetti House and offer to wash the pots. I would take a big soapy pot and go out in the backyard with the pots because they shared the yard with Café Bohemia. That way I could hear the George Wallington Quartet, who practically lived there. Then I went over to Mona's on the corner of Sixth Avenue and MacDougal, right across from Tony Pastor's. My job at Mona's was to get the exotic dancers cabs. Tango, for example, would shake-dance and sit on the laps of sailors, just do her thing, then rip off the wig and bra and, of course, she's a dude. People would get really angry. So my job was to keep a cab at the curb. I would get paid two dollars a night for this.

Another place I worked a lot was the Open Door, where we used to go to hear Miles. I didn't go to hear Miles; I went to see his wardrobe, because he had gorgeous clothes. He always played into the drapes and showed complete contempt for the audience. In the Village I began to run across designers and theater people, artist types, bohemians who had some politics and kind of knew what was happening. But it wasn't until the sixties struck that I really finally felt at home in the world. I finally reconnected with a lot of things from childhood that I had lost. I had lost an edge somewhere while doing those college years, hanging out in Flushing. I always take Harlem as my standard of a viable community: a Speakers' Corner, a place where politics are discussed and where there is critical response so that you do not become captive; a black bookstore so you do not become captive to schools and other indoctrinating institutions; a library in case you can't get to the bookstore; a park to sit at and talk (also, the park can be where Pop Johnson and his cronies sit to create community sovereignty; they can check out who is coming up the walk); you have got to have a screening room of some kind so you can know what our cultural workers are doing with our image and our voice; you have to have a press to get the word out.

Harlem became my standard, and very few neighborhoods fit this. When we moved to South Jamaica, for example, I thought my brain would atrophy. The only thing that came close to a truth-speaking vehicle there was the movie marquee on Merrick Boulevard. The guy who would slot the letters in had a real serious thing about black stars. So, you would get *Casablanca* starring Dooley Wilson, *Pinky* starring Ethel Waters, *Island in the Sun* starring Dandridge and Belafonte, *Spartacus* starring Woody Strode. That was about it, though. Not enough to keep the mind alive.

LM: Going into movies, how are movies part of your development, and how do you begin to interact with them?

TCB: Growing up in Harlem, we had five movie houses in our neighborhood. There was the Dorset, where we saw Boston Blackie and the Three Stooges. That was on Broadway. On Amsterdam, it was the Washington, where we saw sepia movies and second-string things. There was the Sunset and the Regal on 125th Street, where we saw race movies. That's where I saw Herb Jeffries in *Bronze Buckaroo*. On Broadway and 145th Street, there was the RKO Hamilton, where we saw first-run Hollywood movies, as well as a vaudeville show, as well as a bouncing ball sing-along with the corny songs. I was always in the movie house. I liked movies, and I would sit there and rewrite them. Most of the time the stories were stupid because none of the women ever had girlfriends. I used to think, Well, no wonder. No wonder Barbara Stanwyck is getting thrown off the cliff, or Lana Turner is getting shot, or Bette Davis is having hysterics. They don't have any girlfriends. When the story was really dumb, I would start looking at the scenic design: I like that ashtray; I wonder where they got that color. Oh, the clothes in *Mata Hari*. When I first said to myself, I'm going to make movies when I grow up, was in the Apollo. In the Apollo between shows, would be these god-awful shorts with petrochemical eye-stinging colors that blurred outside of the outlines. They were about such really fascinating subjects as the tin can industry. I used to think, Damn, when I grow up, I'm going to make really great shorts for the Apollo. I didn't understand that they were deliberately chosen to get you out of there. They are called "chasers." So you would get up, get out, and the people outside on line could come in and a new show could start. I didn't know that. I just thought somebody didn't have any taste and were buying these really awful movies. That was the first conscious notion of wanting to become a filmmaker.

Then in 1964 I refused to go to work. I'm hanging down in the Village in the early morning. I walk by the Greenwich movie house and the guy is up on the ladder putting up the letters and it says, "Two African films by Ousmane Sembène." I thought, Sembène, I've been reading Sembène. I go over and look at the glossies and they are playing *Borom Sarret* and *La Femme Noire*. I had never thought about African movies. So I went in to see them, and I stayed and saw them again. I figured I might not see them again, and also my friends haven't, so I have to memorize every shot, and then I'll play it out for buddies. Now *Borom Sarret* really resonated with me because I was working on a story called "Sanitary Belt," as in "Cordon Sanitaire," about that hedgerow built as a barrier between European quarters and native quarters. I was playing around with the notion of belt in general, conveyor belt, on the line, worker in the factory, warehousing of Africans, etc.

In Sembène's film there is this Cordon Sanitaire, and that sparked me. I came out of there very late at night. I was in there all day studying those movies. I was studying every frame because I did not think I would ever see them again. It was then I thought I might go to Africa and become a filmmaker. Then in 1970, shortly after my *Black Woman* book came out, and shortly after Chester H. Higgins, Jr.'s first book of photographs came out, we met each other up at the Studio Museum; and we decided to take the film course with Randy Abbott and Ngaio Killingsworth. I wanted to learn editing. Everybody else wanted to go out in the street with equipment. I knew that a film is made in the editing room, and I wanted to be in there. I studied editing under Ngaio and Randy, and we had lots of footage to play with because everybody went out in the street, shot stuff, and gave it up. I could have made fifty movies with all that footage. I was up there having a wonderful time at the Studio Museum learning editing. Of course, by 1970 we'd heard of the UCLA rebellion, the Watts films, Charlie Burnett, and that whole crew. We heard about the overturning of the school curriculum at the film school. They wanted to make films out in the streets, in the community. I thought that was fabulous.

On the East Coast there was the war to get WNET on board and for black folks to get in the door, and there were a lot of documentaries being made. St. Clair Bourne was working as a filmmaker and as editor of *Chamba Notes*. Pearl Bowser was doing a black retrospective film festival at the Jewish Museum. The idea really began to take hold. Then I moved to Atlanta in 1974. Louis Bilaggi Bailey and Richard Hudlin (kin to the Hudlin brothers) were programming independent black films, and every once in a while a filmmaker would come through and we would show films at my house because I had a big old sloppy house and I didn't care if you moved things around and dropped things. Bailey founded the Atlanta Annual Third World Film Festival, an attempt to program films from around the world. The Festival became a genuinely international event when Cheryl Chisholm took over as director.

I began programming with the notion that eventually I would get around to making movies, would back myself into it. Then I came to Philadelphia and met Louis Massiah, founder-director of the Scribe Video Center. Louis had just come back from Mali. He had done a lot of videos and was thinking about another one. I suggested he tackle the "Move incident" as a community-voice video. He called me up and invited me to come down and do the narration. I thought, Narration . . . great. I sit in a booth, like Ernest Hemingway with *Spanish Earth*, and I watch the film, jot down notes, and then record. He didn't tell me that I had to write the script, help him devise the film, *and* narrate! Which was wonderful, actually. So now I am based at the Scribe Video Center in Philadelphia and helping to develop filmmakers. I work as a production facilitator for Louis's project called Community Visions, where we aid community-based organizations to explore video as an instrument for social change. I also teach script writing there, and every time I teach a workshop I write a script to make sure I know what I'm talking about. By now I've got this huge folio of scripts, which ends all excuses, so this spring I will start working on a couple of films.

LM: We are missing the writing, which is absolutely essential. Could you talk about the genesis of *The Black Woman*? How did that come about?
TCB: In 1968 I was teaching at City College in the SEEK program.

LM: What was the SEEK Program?

TCB: The SEEK program was "Let's get these colored people in here, let them fail and flunk out so we don't have to be bothered with them again." But a number of us managed to get up there. The attrition rate at City College was something like fourteen percent, and in the SEEK Program it was less than nine. We were very serious. There was me, Addison Gayle, Barbara Christian, Audre Lorde, June Jordan, Larry Neal. It was a heavy bunch of folk up there at that time. Three people got on my case. One was Francine Covington, a student I greatly admired, and a woman I greatly admire today. I loved her style of confrontation. She would say to me, "You've been saying this, that, and the other. Why don't you do a book, damnit?" That made me think.

Then Dan Watts, editor of *The Liberator*, where I did book reviews and so forth, said, "You have an interesting take on things. You ought to write a book." Then Addison Gayle would say, "I heard you deliver eight talks. Why the hell don't you write them down and get them printed?" I thought, Oh, a book about black women. That would be great. I had read a piece by Rudy Doris about women and leadership and SNCC, so I talked to the women in the Panther party, women in CORE, women in SNCC. They were writing position papers and taking the brothers to task for their foolishness and shit. I wanted to get some papers out of them and put them in a book. But the women said, "No, this is in-house stuff. We are not interested in going public." I thought that was a shame and I said, "I'll wait." So, from 1968 to 1969 I am waiting for this call. Then I began looking around for an agent, and I found Cyrilly Abels, an old European-American leftist woman. We began going around to the publishing houses and I began running into a lot of people I used to go to school with, white folks. They are saying things like, "I've seen fabulous manuscripts from black women, but they wind up on the sludge pile because there is no market for black women's works." So then I got this idea: Never mind the papers from the Panther party women; let me do a book that will kick the door open. I know there is a market for black women's work out there because I know 800 million black women all by myself. Nikki Giovanni gave me a poem, Alice Childress gave me a story. I put together this anthology that I felt would open the door and prove that there was a market. Sure enough, within the second month the book came out, it went into a new edition. That book was everywhere. There were pyramids of *The Black Woman* in every bookstore. All I knew in the beginning was that it had to fit in your pocket and it had to be under a dollar. I didn't know anything about publishing, but I stuck to that. After it came out, a number of startling things happened. My attention at that time was on kicking the door open so that other black women's manuscripts could get a hearing, and they certainly did. People then began calling me to do lectures and workshops on women's issues. I didn't know anything so I had to study a lot and call up a lot of people. Alice Childress was very good to me in those years. She was one of the first people who walked up to me, put her hands on my shoulders and said, "You have done something valuable. Now, watch out." That was very valuable. The Harlem Writer's Guild gave me a party and I thought that was going to be the end of it. But no, then came all these urgings to be a particular kind of person, an expert, a spokeswoman. I was having trouble being a public person.

Next, I did an anthology called *Tales and Stories for Black Folks* that came out in 1971. What I love about that book is that my students are in it. I was teaching at Rutgers in those days, and one of the things I always tried to make clear to students was "Do not write term papers for me. Make sure they are useful for somebody else as well." People began to write position papers for organizations in their community. A number of people were working at the storytelling library hour, so they wrote stories. I thought that the stories were great and I published them in the book. That book didn't stay in print very long. I was at the Livingston campus of Rutgers then, and everybody on campus had a copy of the book.

LM: What was the impact of *Gorilla, My Love* on your life?
TCB: One of my good girlfriends in those days was Hattie Gossett. In those days we were all piecing a living together. Hattie said, "Hey, let me be your agent." She told me about a woman up at Random House named Toni Morrison who was very interested in my work. I said, "Oh, yeah?" She said, "Put together a book and I'll sell it." So I pulled out a bunch of stuff from under the mattress, from the bottom drawer, the trunks, and I spread all this stuff around and I thought, Ooh, a collection. I thought I would put together stories that show my different voices. It looked good, but it looked like ten people wrote this thing. I went to the library and read a bunch of collections and noticed that the voice was consistent, but it was a boring and monotonous voice. Oh, your voice is supposed to be consistent in a collection, I figured. Then I pulled out a lot of stories that had a young protagonist-narrator because that voice is kind of consistent—a young, tough, compassionate girl. Then I changed my mind because the salesmen at the publishing house will think my book is a juvenile book for a juvenile market only. So I put some adult stuff in.

Then at that time I was writing a play called *The Johnson Girls*, which we performed on the *Soul!* show with Audreen Ballard in the role of Inez. Now it is becoming a film with Barbara O done by Iverson White. I decided to adapt the play as a story, and that became one of the stories in *Gorilla, My Love*. Miss Morrison didn't touch anything. She sort of floats a few ideas at you and whispers in that gentle way. Then you go home and think, Oh, brain surgery! Let me rewrite. The book came out, and I never dreamed that such a big fuss would be made. "Oh, *Gorilla, My Love*, what a radical use of dialect! What a bold, political angle on linguistics!" At first I felt like a fraud. It didn't have anything to do with a political stance. I just thought people lived and moved around in this particular language system. It is also the language system I tend to remember childhood in. This is the language many of us speak. It just seemed polite to handle the characters in this mode. I never knew how to answer, so I would just let people talk about the book. I began to learn what was in that book and what was so different and distinct about it.

LM: You have traveled extensively around the world. You have been to Cuba, Sweden, Vietnam, Laos, India, Nigeria, Jamaica, Barbados. You have often traveled as a delegate. What is that experience like, and why is that important to you?

TCB: When you are member of a delegation, you have responsibility before you go, while you are there, and when you come back. Before you go, you want to contact your constituency and find out what they want to know about that country. Also, what kind of solidarity they wish to express with the people of that country, and what sort of materials they would like to send. For example, when we went to Cuba, we took diaphragms, blood plasma, and penicillin. When folks went to Guinea-Bissau, building materials. To Brazil, mops, because none of the maids have mops. In the spring of 1975 I was part of a delegation called the North American Academic Marxist-Leninist Anti-Imperialist Feminist Women. It used to take us ten minutes to introduce ourselves. We were invited by the Women's Union of North Vietnam to come as a delegation and to do what delegates do, like raising critical questions such as: What was the infant mortality rate before the Revolution? What is it now? What was the rate of literacy before the Revolution? What is it now? Who were the people on the bottom strata, and what position do they hold now? What are their prospects for the next ten years? I was always interested in the personal stories and I would ask, "Who were you then and who are you now?" We were invited in the spring to go to Vietnam, but they had the victory in the spring, which was unexpected, so the Women's Union needed to go around and visit the socialist camp and thank people for their solidarity during the struggle. So we were put on hold. Many of us had already quit our jobs, sublet our apartments, turned off our phones, etc. I sat down and wrote, and that became *The Sea Birds*. Most of those stories had not been published; been hanging around the house, and they were completed during that spring and summer.

In Vietnam we were also interested in bringing back things for our constituency; we would have to give a debriefing and a report of some kind and had to shape it in some palatable way. Children gave us cards to give to the children here expressing solidarity. When I got back, one of the tasks I had was to deliver this information to my constituency. I decided to do it the way I knew how to do. I wrote a short story in seven sections. I would read a section, then we would have music, somebody would get up and read the greeting cards that the children had made. Then I would read another section based on stories I had been told, then someone would show some slides and posters, then I would read another section. It went on like that. That story line became the title story in *The Sea Birds Are Still Alive*. Very oddly the first time I ever heard it on radio, the person read it, and then had music, then read it, etc. I thought it must really lend itself to that kind of orchestration.

LM: You were in Atlanta when you were writing *The Salt Eaters*—could you talk about that?

TCB: *The Salt Eaters*, like many works, started as entries in my journal. I was trying to figure out as a community worker why political folk were so distant from the spiritual community—clairvoyants, mediums, those kind of folks, whom I was always studying with. I wondered what would happen if we could bring them together as Bookman brought them together under Toussaint, as Nan brought them together in Jamaica. Why is there that gap? Why don't we have a bridge language so that clairvoyants can talk to revolutionaries? So I began thinking about it and jotting things down in my journal. Then the entries got very long; then they threatened to turn into a story. I had hoped that the story would be a short story since I don't have staying power. It was going to be about either a Mardi Gras society or a samba school. This society, for some kind of festival, would elect to reenact an old slave insurrection. They do so, and all hell breaks loose because of the objective conditions in that area. I thought I could pull that off in seventeen pages. I began working on it and it got to be a novel. It was very difficult sledding because I was writing quite beyond myself in a number of ways. I was writing that book in 1981 so I could kick cancer's ass in 1993. That book taught me how to get well. If I hadn't written it, I'm not quite sure I'd be sitting here. I was writing beyond myself in that sense.

Also in the sense that I was stretching, reaching, trying to do justice to that realm of reality that we all live in but do not acknowledge, because the English language is for mercantile business and not for the interior life. The only time you see that realm rendered is in science fiction. I was trying to find another way to do it, and I think I did. So I was writing beyond myself in that sense. When I look at that book now, I realize I'm not there yet. I don't understand it yet. It resonates, it chimes in my bones, but I don't understand it yet. It was very hard work. It is a breathless book. When Morrison got a hold of it, I thought that she would take care of it. "Ahh, she'll fix it." She didn't touch it. She said, "This is fine." I said, "Really?" She said, "Yes." I waited for her to whisper at me, I waited for her to drift some stuff across my brainpan, but she didn't, she left the book alone. Or, rather, she whispered so softly I didn't know what was prompting the rewrites.

When the book came out, there was a weird reaction to it. Some reviews were very favorable but totally uninformed. Some reviews were not favorable but informed. I got wonderful mail from people who said, "Thank you for breaking this ground because I want to write like this, but I don't want to write science fiction. I like this alternative reality. Thank you." Other people wrote, "'The Yellow Wallpaper' room taught me that I needed to get well. *The Salt Eaters* taught me how." I got letters from various people who are now friends, from the Asian community, the Chicana community, who picked up on the Seven Sisters—Women of the Rice, Women of the Plantation, Women of the Corn, who said, "We must all get together and create a Seven Sisters collective. We must do an opera." I am continually haunted by the Seven Sisters. In the late fifties I wrote a story called "The Talking Stick." It was about a study group called the Seven Sisters. In *The Salt Eaters* the Seven Sisters are a performing troupe. In a bunch of things I am doing now, called *Goddess Sightings*, the Seven Sisters are a network of people in North America, South America, and Central America, and they get together to do things like reimagine America. *The Salt Eaters* was usable, apparently; I kept finding quotes from it everywhere. People started quoting sections of it in their speeches. I would find quotes on greeting cards—which nobody paid me for. Carole Parks, with permission, used it to create a conference calendar with quotes for each month. Other people drew maps of the landscapes and the worlds in it and turned them into T-shirts for which I was not paid.

Then folks started teaching it. Charles Frye taught a course in ethics in the philosophy department at Mount Holyoke and this was the required text. He called me up and asked me to come speak. I am not a silly woman, so I said, "If you want to conduct an intelligent discussion, you call Eleanor Traylor. I don't know nothing about the book. I'm still reading it." I am still catching up with the wisdom of that book.

LM: In particular, and in general, how has motherhood and how has Karma, your daughter, affected your work?

TCB: It is very hard to answer. One of the things that Karma did very early in life when people would call me was to say, "She's busy. She's out of it. She is staring out the window. But she's working." They must have said, "Well, this is important." She would say, "Is it important to you or important to her?" I said, "I like this kid. I'm keeping this kid. This kid understands." Then they would probably say something she didn't like, and she would hang up and say, "Some people are so rude to children." Karma gave me permission to write, in the sense that she would not disturb me if I was in my particular chair, at my particular table. She would move around me and take care of things.

There was a period too when I went utterly mad in the eighties in response to the Atlanta missing and murdered children's case. That manuscript too started as journal entries and then developed into pieces that I did for the newspapers, and then I finally realized that I had a novel on my hands, and I didn't want it. One of the reasons I didn't want it was because I knew too much, and I thought if I could reconstruct the real case, and know the difference between this and that highly selective media-police-city-hall-fiction on which someone got convicted, how safe am I? Everybody in the world was doing research for me. People from *Newsweek* and *60 Minutes* would call me up and ask me, "Do you have another angle on this?" I would look in my notes, I would look at something I hadn't researched yet, and I would say, "Yeah, why don't you check out this and get back to me." I didn't have to leave my house. As a result, I stopped going out, I stopped bathing, I stopped washing my hair, I became this lunatic. My daughter would tap me every now and then and say, "Ma, you look like hell." Then it was "Mother, get it together." She was thirteen at the time, and she took what little money was left and enrolled in the Barbizon Modeling School; the idea was to make money as a runway model, pay the bills, and keep us going until I found myself again. She has been a tremendous support in writing. If your children give you permission to write, that's heavy. I am now in a period of recovery, and so is she, so our talk is very interesting. She was remarking the other day that she had no idea that all the skills that she had developed taking care of my sorry ass, that these were marketable skills.

It was Cheryl Chisholm down in Atlanta who hired her to do some work for the film festival that called on many of those homemade skills. She is very good at cleaning off desks, booking your trips, getting people off the phone, blocking people at the door. She is really a good caretaker. When Julie Dash sent out an SOS, Karma went in there and took care of Julie and helped her get the book out. People praise her and she looks at me and shrugs, "Well, it's just what I did with you."

LM: What's the present phase, particularly in light of your bout with cancer in 1993?

TCB: For several years I had been stuck—spiritually, financially, psychically, physically. Finally my intestines were blocked. I knew I had been blocked because I couldn't feel my spirit guides around me. I would meditate and get rocked by earthquakes and thunderstorms and all kinds of stuff that never happened before. I was not growing as a creative person. I was putting that kind of sacred practice on the back burners, wrenching my way away from a path I knew I was supposed to take. I knew that I had cancer. So when the doctor told me I had cancer, I already knew.

Now I am in the process of recovery, physically, financially, psychically, spiritually. I am coming through it slowly, mainly by trying to get down to those chambers where I work when I am at my best. No matter what the work is, there is a place I can go to when I am in touch with the best of myself, and I am connected with the most powerful something or others—spirit guides—let's call them angels, if you like. I also have a tremendous feeling of attachment to friends all over who are the people who got me out of that bed and got me well. I was talking to my surgeon the other day, who was, as usual, praising himself about his scalpel. I pointed out, once again, "Your scalpel is only a physical manifestation of the love and affection of my friends. They got me off the table." When I was in bed, just whipped, but I had something to do, I would reach everywhere for energy and nothing would happen. But all of a sudden I would get this surge of energy, and I would be up, walking down the ward, giving away my flowers, talking to people, giving orders. Then someone would call, and I would find out that they had been at a prayer group at that moment, or two or three people had lit some candles at that moment to send me some energy. So I am in the period of recovery, and please do light candles for me because I need some help. I am trying to write things I have never written before, again writing beyond myself. I am doing a series of things called *Goddess Sightings*. Some of them are stories, some of them are obviously scripts for video or film, and one of them will be an installation and performance piece as part of Miss Morrison's Atelier project at Princeton. I am going to do a garden of goddesses and film it.

LM: Can you talk about your voice lessons?
TCB: One of the aspects of my recovery is that I am taking vocal lessons, which have enabled me to free my voice on many levels. I always thought I lived out loud, but I didn't. It also is helping me breathe on many levels. My teacher is a yoga teacher as well. I decided to take lessons after I came back from the National Black Arts Festival in Atlanta. I had the best time down there. I went down there for a gig, and I just stayed on. When I came home, I felt, Why can't we all feel like that all the time? I was told that when I stopped chemo I might go into depression; it shapes your week, getting ready for it, recovering from chemo, defending the immune system, etc. So I needed to be into something before I started. Well, I was always threatening to take singing lessons. So I have been taking singing lessons. We do drills, breathing exercises, I sing, I do yoga, I do German lieder and Italian arias and Cole Porter. It is very much a part of my recovery.

LM: Are there any questions?

Q: What does the expression you use, "Sam Browne belt," mean?
TCB: It is a thick, ugly Texas ranger belt. It is mean and fascist, and it hurts bad. Michael's mother was a severe little woman who wore severe clothes, and she would beat that boy with that belt.

Q: I wanted to ask about your expression in dance and movement.
TCB: In reclaiming the body from the biomedical syndicate as well as from the naturopathic types I have been dealing with, the best way I know of recovering the body is movement. It is only when I am dancing that I inhabit all of my body. When I was in academia, that life would drive me up into my mouth, and all of me would be huddled behind my teeth, and I would have to remind myself that I have this space to stretch out in. When I am totally in my body, I know it, because when I run into people, all of me remembers them. My thigh remembers them, my mind is everywhere, and also I feel gigantic. When I walk down the street, I feel very large, physically as well

as spiritually. I feel like everybody is a friend of mine and everybody is just wonderful: "God, it's going to be great when we finally take over and be in charge of this yard. Kente cloth in the Oval Office, deviled eggs on the menu, peach cobbler on the lawn." I have no idea what movement I will get into because my girlfriend Arlene said to me, "So-and-so, the African drummer, is going to be at the Center." I said, "So what?" She said, "I'll pick you up at ten o'clock and we'll go." I thought we were going to watch. Around nine-thirty she called and said, "What are you wearing?" I said, "I've got my pajamas on." She said, "We're going to the dance class." I said, "Are you serious? I am lucky I can walk." Anyway, I got into my tights, the leg warmers, and I went to the dance class.

Now, even when I had been in the best of shape and thought I was a dancer, I never could get through a class. I am flashy and have a lot of presence and style, but no technique. People put me in the front line in the beginning because I am a quick study, but after about fifteen minutes I begin to flag so they put me in the back and I start falling apart. This class was fast; they had some serious drummers. They were reaching that tempo when you get scared—the horses are coming! The drummers kept coming up to that threshold rhythm and I kept getting nervous. Do you know what I mean? Trance drumming to summon the loa. I am trying to dance and it was awful. It was just pitiful. Miss Dunham would've shot me. I am not sure what movement I will go into now. I have done Alexander technique, I've done Nikolai technique, I've done gymnastics. My daughter has done tae kwon do and the like. I'm thinking maybe I'll go that route. In Philadelphia there are any number of us who are doing movement, such as Sandy Clark Smith and Denise Sneed, so I will check with them.

Q: Political concerns have always been a big part of your life. Have you felt any personal disorientation from what has happened in the world in the last few years in terms of the collapse of some of the models we looked up to? Do you still feel in terms of your own sense of what struggle has to be for us here in this country, do you feel that sense of struggle is still very much intact and has not been destabilized by any of these developments?

TCB: Yes, I'm disoriented and yes, I do think it has been destabilized, and what I have done in response to it is to close in. I don't do nearly the kind of work I used to do. My arena is very limited. I am still doing draft counseling; I work with women from the Persian Gulf thing. What I am always telling them is that they have to do a video and get their stories out. If I can't do it in video, I don't want to do it. If there is any work that people call me for, if it doesn't involve video I won't do it, because I need to focus and not get too scattered. I think it is because of a lack of courage; there is nothing noble about it, so don't clap. When I go to places or meet people I assume are still struggling and find out they are not, it is very depressing, so I just stay where I am with like-minded people. I can affect and create some value where I am.

Q: I have noticed that none of the African American films that I have seen have been taken from great American literature. How you do feel about films made by whites about blacks?
TCB: They are ugly; we don't need them, we have our own genius. *Nothing but a Man*, despite the stupid title, is an exception.

Q: How do you feel about Hollywood films in general?
TCB: I don't feel anything about them. I don't have to because I am very deeply steeped in the independent sector. I don't have to go get mugged all the time. I go to movies constantly because I am a film nut. But I go to see them to train myself in film, to look at what are the conventional practices, and what do they mean ideologically or politically, and how to avoid them. When I go to movies to enjoy and to blossom, I'm going to independent films, in particular independent black films, but also independent Asian films, the independent films that are being conducted in that sector away from the industry, that do not take the Hollyweird model as the protocol, but rather are striking out for something else, for a socially responsible cinema. That's where I am. I don't have many expectations from Hollywood. They can tolerate certain kinds of criticism, but they do not tolerate another vision. If you have a different vision, you need to be moving in the independent sector.

Q: Are there any films that you want to recommend?
TCB: *Sankofa* and the Du Bois documentary called *W. E. B. Du Bois: A Biography in Four Voices*, and also *The KKK Boutique Ain't Just Rednecks*.

Index

www.ingramcontent.com/pod-product-compliance
Lightning Source LLC
Chambersburg PA
CBHW020659030726
47498CB00002B/574